THE
STUDENT
ORIENTAL
COOK BOOK

First published in Great Britain in 1994
by Collins & Brown Limited
London House
Great Eastern Wharf
Parkgate Road
London SW11 4NQ

1 3 5 7 9 8 6 4 2

British Library Cataloguing-in-Publication Data:
A catalogue record for this book
is available from the British Library.

ISBN 1 85585 214 4

Conceived, edited and designed by Collins & Brown Limited

Editors: Catherine Ward and Ruth Baldwin

Art Director: Roger Bristow

Designed by: Claire Graham

Typeset by Textype Typesetters
Printed and bound in
Finland by WSOY

THE STUDENT ORIENTAL COOK BOOK

Eating well without mixer,
microwave or money

Sarah Freeman

COLLINS & BROWN

• ACKNOWLEDGEMENTS •

Many people have helped with this book in one way or another and I want to thank them all very sincerely. Those who supplied ideas or recipes have been credited in the relevant places, but I am particularly grateful to Shehzad Hussein, Shobhna and Kumud Shah (who are not related), Yan-kit So, and also to the chefs David Eyre and Hugo Arnold, who kindly gave me recipes which in the event I could not use. In addition, I owe an enormous debt to the students who tested the recipes, notably Claudia Townsend, Imogen Stanfield, Amy Spurling and, above all, Alex Freeman, whose exceptional talent and precision have been invaluable throughout the progress of the book.

Others whom I wish to thank are Dodie Miller of the Cool Chile Company, Marks & Spencer PLC and Harvey Nichols & Co., who provided information on ingredients. I am also very grateful to Ruth Baldwin, who copy-edited the book, and to Sarah Hoggett and Catherine Ward of Collins & Brown, not only for suggestions and advice but for their kindness, enthusiasm and humour, which have turned hard work into a constant pleasure. Finally, I want to express particular appreciation of my husband, who has lived continuously on rice and spices (as he did pasta last year) and never failed to comment honestly and constructively.

. CONTENTS .

• INTRODUCTION •

As always, I shall make this introduction as short as I can – not least because the more space it takes up, the less there is for recipes. The idea of the *Student Cook Books* was originally suggested by a group of students who wanted to be able to produce really good meals despite lack of money and having little or no experience in the kitchen. As well as lack of money was the limitation of time, not only for cooking but also for shopping. For this reason, and because some of them were studying in places without specialist shops, they agreed that as far as possible ingredients should be restricted to goods stocked by the major supermarket chains. Other conditions which they felt were important were that only basic kitchen equipment should be taken for granted; that all the recipes, except those for sauces and puddings, should be for complete one-dish meals; and that as well as being good in the gastronomic sense, dishes should be nutritionally well balanced and healthy. To ensure that the recipes were really what they wanted, each was tried by at least one member of a very honest and critical student testing team and any which was found to be too difficult, expensive or, above all, did not inspire whole-hearted enthusiasm in terms of taste was thrown out or altered.

The present book (the fourth in the series) is planned along exactly the same lines. However, with this one I feel the need to stress that I have had to balance practical considerations – such as cost, availability of ingredients and the condition of one-dish meals – against the often conflicting demands of authenticity. In the interest of authenticity I asked two Indian cooks in particular to contribute recipes: Shehzad Hussein and Shobhna Shah. Also, although I have tried to avoid using goods which are not sold in supermarkets, I have included a few carefully selected items for which you may have to go to an Oriental store: all except one (dried mushrooms, which I have used only twice) are fairly cheap.

Another point which I feel needs stressing is that the length of some of the recipes does not mean that they are difficult. I know that I have said this in every introduction so far, but on looking through the contents of the book I feel obliged to repeat myself. The use of spices accounts for the large number of ingredients in many Indian recipes; that the directions are often rather long is because I have explained every step in detail for the benefit of inexperienced cooks.

Two minor changes to the contents of the book are a chapter on basic preparations and accompaniments at the beginning, and another on sweet dishes with rice which I could not resist adding, if only as an illustration of the diversity of ways in which rice can be used. In a small book like this, it has been impossible to do justice to its adaptability. Similarly, I have been able to offer no more than a brief introduction to the styles of cooking included, two of which – Indian and Chinese – are among the oldest and most sophisticated in the world.

• INGREDIENTS •

Vegetables and Herbs In both the last two books I have begun this section with the same message: the importance of freshness. When I go to Chinese stores I am always struck by the displays of vegetables, not because of their difference in kind or variety from Western produce, but because of their pristine condition – they look as if they had been picked or pulled only half an hour before. Of course, it would be interesting to use (for instance) long beans, which can be up to a metre in length, but Western stringless beans are an excellent substitute if you can find them in the same state of snappy crispness; the same applies to other items.

For reasons of texture and flavour, I have included stringless beans in a number of recipes despite the fact that they are relatively expensive. However, they are better value than they seem because of the lack of wastage in terms of stalk or outside leaves. I have used only small quantities: if you have to buy them in 225-g/7-oz packs at your local supermarket, go to a greengrocer who will probably sell them loose. A cheaper option than French or Kenya beans is green haricot, which are larger but, if young and fresh, very crisp.

In the past I have been criticized for recommending fresh herbs, which I know are expensive and often difficult to buy:

for these reasons I suggested growing your own. This time I have used only three: mint, coriander (with one or two options of dill and parsley) and lemon grass, which is East Asian and may have to be bought from specialist shops, although it is sometimes sold in supermarkets. Coriander is needed constantly: growing it helps, but as one small plant can supply only a limited amount, you will almost certainly have to buy some on occasion. Packs from supermarkets cost around 50 p; if stored in the refrigerator, they should keep for at least 2 days. It is usually cheaper to buy herbs loose from greengrocers; however, coriander wilts very quickly. Wash it in cold water as soon as possible and store in the refrigerator in an airtight bag. Loose mint also wilts and should be treated in the same way. Lemon grass is a bulb which looks like a spring onion and has a strong lemon-sherbet taste; if similarly kept chilled, it will stay fresh for at least 10 days. Like other herbs it can be bought dried, but the dried version tastes like hay. If you cannot buy fresh lemon grass, use lemon peel.

Spices The spices needed in this book are: cloves and cinnamon; cardamom, which is highly aromatic and very characteristic of Indian cookery; coriander seeds (as opposed to leaves), which have a slightly peppery, orange-like flavour; cumin, which is pungent and slightly bitter; fennel, which tastes of anise and is still more pungent; black and white mustard seeds (hot: black is hottest); turmeric, which is mildly aromatic and dyes ingredients yellow; saffron, which is more strongly aromatic and also dyes items yellow; plus vanilla, ground ginger and chilli powder. All can be bought at supermarkets and all, except saffron and vanilla, both of which I have used only once, are fairly cheap. Saffron is the stigma of a crocus which has to be hand-picked; the cost of vanilla, which is a pod, is due to processing.

As spices rapidly lose their aroma and much of their flavour after grinding, all except turmeric, ground ginger and chilli powder, which are useful for particular purposes, should be bought whole and crushed, if necessary, before use. This sounds like a sentence of hard labour, but it is not, because where they are used extensively – that is, in Indian cookery – they are left whole whenever practicable, adding a nutty texture to the dish. Powdered saffron and vanilla essence are cheaper than the stigmas and pods: vanilla essence, however, tastes of chemicals, and powdered saffron of almost nothing, although it serves as a very effective dye.

Salt and Pepper Although you may not be accustomed to thinking of them as such, salt and pepper can also be counted as spices and are similarly preferable unground. Buy black peppercorns and crush them in a mortar if you have no mill, and use unpowdered sea-salt crystals. I especially recommend Maldon salt, which has a soft, subtle flavour and only needs crushing with the back of a spoon.

Ginger and Chillies I should really have discussed ginger and chillies under the heading of vegetables because, although spices when dried, they are vegetables when fresh and are used in their fresh form in most of the recipes in this book. Ground and root ginger are different articles which can seldom be satisfactorily interchanged. Green chillies are fresh by their nature (if kept and dried, they will redden). I have stated 'fresh red chillies' when red chillies are needed, but if you cannot find them or the ones you buy turn out to have no heat, used dried ones instead.

Chillies present a problem even to the expert shopper because of their variations in heat. There are over 150 kinds, some of which are easily identifiable, others not. However, knowing which sort you are buying is not always helpful, since strength may differ within the kinds and sometimes between chillies from the same plant. An importer who is trying to introduce a wider range into this country, Dodie Miller, advises tasting before buying or, if this is impossible because the chillies are pre-packed, checking on the country of origin: those from Thailand or South America will probably be hot. In any case I suggest tasting before cooking: you need only bite a very tiny piece. A hot chilli can also be detected by smell and the fact that chopping it causes your eyes to smart. Heat can be adjusted according to the dish and your taste not only by using fewer or more actual chillies but by discarding or including their seeds, which add considerably to their strength.

Curry Powder This has its uses, but the mention of it will cause Indian cooks to shrink. To them, starting with powder is like putting the cart before the horse: part of the art of their cooking is to suit the spices to the particular dish. If you adopt their practice of using spices whole, curry powder will not save much time either. I have therefore included no recipes for making it or dishes using it. However, I have given a recipe for an aromatic spice mixture, garam masala, which is sometimes used as a finishing touch to dishes (see page 21).

Coconuts and Coconut Products A sweet, fresh coconut will have more flavour than the processed versions, but unfortunately, just as you cannot be certain of the heat of chillies, so you cannot count on the flavour of coconuts. All you can do is to check that they are free of mould and heavy, which means that they contain plenty of liquid. I may have been unlucky, but of the last eight apparently sound ones that I have bought, one had excellent flavour, one was rancid and the remaining six had decidedly less taste than desiccated coconut.

Desiccated coconut can be used when the grated nut is called for or to make milk (see page 24), for which in general I recommend it despite the greater convenience of other products, namely coconut cream, coconut milk powder and tinned milk. However, tinned milk, which is thick, is a good choice for puddings (see pages 141–150). Milk powder has the advantage that you can make it up to the thickness and in the quantity required, but it has a slightly artificial taste, perhaps because of the chemicals needed to keep it free-flowing. A fresh nut and 250 g/8 oz desiccated coconut (which represents the contents of an average fresh nut) each cost around 50 p, 400-ml/⅔-pint tins about 75 p, and a 150-g/5-oz packet of powder approximately 87 p.

Poultry and Eggs Both on humanitarian grounds and in the interest of taste, I have assumed throughout the book that you will use free-range chicken and eggs: even with the extra cost, they represent remarkable value.

• OTHER INGREDIENTS •

For most of the recipes in this book, you will need groundnut (peanut) oil; for deep-frying I have recommended corn oil; and for some Indian dishes ghee (clarified butter: see pages 20–21), which is expensive but adds a wonderful richness of flavour. To reduce the cost, I have only used it where it really counts and have often suggested combining it with oil.

As Chinese beancurd is not generally available in this country, I have used Japanese tofu: flavoured varieties can be bought at health-food and other shops, but the recipes here only call for the plain sort widely sold in supermarkets.

Some Chinese-style dishes require medium-dry sherry. I know that this is expensive, but you will not need much for cooking: the rest can be drunk.

Apart from lemon grass, the items that you may have to buy from Oriental shops are oyster sauce, fish sauce, shiitake mushrooms (which are used in only two recipes) and black-bean paste (which is needed only once). Oyster sauce, which contains hardly any oyster and is, in fact, quite cheap, is rich-tasting and slightly sweet; fish sauce is salty and is used in Thai cookery rather as soy is in Chinese. European brands are sold in some supermarkets but I recommend Oriental ones if you can find them. You may not like the smell of the Oriental version when you open the bottle, but I have never met anyone who has not liked the effect when it was added to a dish.

Shiitake mushrooms, black-bean paste and all ingredients not mentioned here are discussed, when necessary, at the heads of recipes.

• STORES •

To reduce odd shopping to the minimum, you should keep supplies of the following:

STORE-CUPBOARD
Basmati and Patna or American long-grain rice (brown or white, but some should be white because it suits all dishes)
Thai fragrant or jasmine rice (white)
Groundnut oil
Ghee
Light soy sauce
Fish sauce
Wine vinegar
Medium-dry sherry
Cornflour
Caster sugar
Coriander, cumin, fennel, and black and white mustard seeds; cinnamon sticks; cardamom pods; black peppercorns; salt; ground ginger and turmeric; hot chilli powder; dried chillies
Desiccated coconut

VEGETABLE RACK
Onions
Fresh root ginger
Garlic
Lemons

REFRIGERATOR/FREEZER
Frozen stock
Frozen peas and sweetcorn
Green chillies

• NUTRITION •

Meals centred on rice are widely regarded as healthy because they contain more starch and less protein and saturated fat than the traditional meat-based European dinner. Often more starch is a good idea; however, it is important not to cut back too far on the protein. I have said this before, but it is worth repeating: meals made up only of rice and vegetables may be satisfying at the time but are unsatisfactory nutritionally. Most vegetables contain very little protein (peas and spinach are exceptions); rice contributes some, but to obtain a useful proportion of your daily requirement you will also have to include a high-protein ingredient, namely meat, fish, dairy products including eggs, pulses, tofu, peas, spinach or nuts (excluding coconut). All the recipes in this book, apart from a few for accompanying dishes or puddings, include at least one of these unless otherwise stated. You should also bear in mind that although rice contains protein, it is considerably less rich in it than wheat. Coconuts (and also chestnuts) contain relatively little: coconut and coconut milk should therefore be treated merely as flavourings and not as the equivalent of other nuts or ordinary milk.

For most people the amount of saturated fat eaten is less important than total fat intake. To readers of this book total fat intake is probably not of immediate concern either, but it is worth pointing out that although I have recommended as little oil as is practicable in the recipes, a certain amount has to be used for curry-type dishes and stir-frying. However, this is, to some extent, offset by the fact that for this type of cooking, meat is usually very carefully trimmed of fat; also, butter and cheese do not go well with Far-Eastern-style dishes in particular. If you eat bread with your meal, you will not want butter; nor, at least in my view, does cheese seem appropriate afterwards.

More information on nutrition and a table of food values are on pages 190–192.

• STORAGE AND HYGIENE •

White rice will keep for up to a year if stored somewhere dry: once packets are opened, put the rice into an airtight jar. Brown rice will keep for only about 2 months, or 3–4 months if placed in an airtight container in the refrigerator. Store oil somewhere cool and dark and spices somewhere cool, dark and dry: for both, a closed cupboard is preferable to an open shelf. Use soy sauce within 6 months: if you want to keep it longer, store it in the refrigerator. Opened bottles of fish and oyster sauce must be kept in the refrigerator and used within 6 weeks.

Store onions and garlic in a cool, dry place: use within 3–4 weeks. In theory you can keep coconuts for some time, but I advise opening them promptly: store the flesh (or milk) in the refrigerator and do not keep for longer than 24 hours. Milk made from desiccated coconut should also be used within 24 hours (see page 23 for preparing fresh coconuts).

Fresh root ginger can be kept outside the refrigerator for 7–10 days or inside for 2–3 weeks: store in a paper bag (foodwrap does not absorb moisture and thus encourages mould). Green or fresh red chillies should similarly be kept chilled in a paper bag: use within 5–7 days. Although herbs and vegetables are best eaten when absolutely fresh, most will keep for 2–3 days in the refrigerator. Stringless beans will last for up to 4 days and celery and carrots can be kept for at least a week, but beans and celery will become tougher and less crisp. All should be left in the packs in which they were bought or stored in sealed food bags. Tomatoes for cooking can be left to ripen at room temperature; potatoes (except very small, new ones) should not be kept chilled but in a dry, dark place. If exposed to bright light, they may develop poisonous green patches on and under the skin which must be peeled off before use.

Put meat, fish, tofu and all dairy products except eggs into the refrigerator as soon as possible after purchase. Note the use-by dates, but cook chicken promptly; use unpackaged meat within 3 days and fish within 1 day. Eggs should be put somewhere cool and used while still very fresh. Cooked rice and spiced or other cooked dishes should be kept chilled and used within 1 day: note that the flavours of spices are unstable and might fade or change. Place dairy products on the top shelf of the refrigerator, cooked dishes on the next, raw meat and fish at the bottom and vegetables in the salad drawer: any which will not fit should go at the top with dairy produce. All items should be covered; try to ensure against leakages and clean out the refrigerator once a week.

Wash your hands before starting to prepare food, before handling salads or crudités and after handling raw eggs, raw meat and other fresh produce, especially chicken. Knives, plates and other utensils used for raw eggs and chicken should similarly be washed directly after use. It is also a good idea to wash eggs before cracking, especially if they are to be separated, in case pieces of shell fall into the contents.

• EQUIPMENT •

I have assumed that you will have access to the following equipment: a cooker and a refrigerator, scales, a colander, a sieve, bowls, knives, spoons, saucepans, a frying-pan and a pestle and mortar. Any other items needed such as perforated spoons, graters, spatulas, casseroles or baking-dishes are given with the recipes.

Often you can manage without scales: weights can be judged from packets, or mugs and tablespoons used as measures: 1 full 300-ml/½-pint mug of uncooked rice = 250 g/ 8 oz; 1 level tablespoon of sugar or 2 tablespoons of flour = 25 g/ 1 oz. Scales, however, are extremely helpful when cooking rice because the proportion of rice to water needs to be fairly exact.

It is also a great advantage to have a wok, partly because it is bowl-shaped: this enables you to push items that are cooking too quickly up the sides, and also means that you need less oil than with a conventional, flat-bottomed frying-pan. I have used a wok for both Indian- and Far-Eastern-style dishes throughout the book and have given amounts of oil accordingly. If you choose to use a saucepan or frying-pan instead, you will need a little extra.

An essential item for cooking rice is a medium-sized or largish saucepan with a lid.

Another essential piece of equipment is a pestle and mortar. I have already lamented the cost of these and suggested, rather feebly, that you persuade somebody to give you one as a present. A conveniently large one, with a mortar about 15 cm/6 inches across, such as I use myself, will cost at least £12; however, I have now discovered that you can buy small but perfectly serviceable ones for about £8. I admit that this is still not very cheap, but at least it makes for a less demanding present.

• PREPARATION AND COOKING TECHNIQUES •

Complete cooking instructions are given with the recipes; here, however, I have made a few additional remarks about processes which recur throughout the book.

SIMMERING
Simmering is cooking in liquid which is just on the point of boiling: the top moves or bubbles a little according to whether you are simmering slowly or fast. However, bubbling should never be more than slight: if the liquid is milk, it should not be hot enough to rise. Adjusting the heat demands care: this applies particularly if the saucepan is to be covered, since you must allow for the fact that adding a lid will raise the temperature inside slightly.

REDUCING
This is the term used for boiling down cooking liquid to condense it until only a little remains. It usually applies to sauces.

SWEATING
In this book, the term 'sweating' is used for drawing juice from watery vegetables by sprinkling them with salt (the word can also be used, however, for frying vegetables very slowly). The vegetable is chopped or grated, sprinkled with fine salt and left, preferably in a sieve or colander, for at least half an hour; the salt should be rinsed off in cold water prior to cooking.

REFRESHING
To refresh is to rinse vegetables in cold water directly after boiling and draining to arrest further cooking: the effect is to keep them crisp and brightly coloured.

PREPARING AND COOKING VEGETABLES
To retain as much as possible of the vitamin content of vegetables, you should not cut them up until just before use (this is not always possible with, say, aubergines or cucumber which have to be left to sweat, but applies as a general rule). For the same reason vegetables should be boiled in the

minimum of water: this also has the advantage of preserving flavour. If the vegetable liquor is only very lightly salted, use it instead of stock for a stir-fried dish.

FRYING SPICES

When spices are added to hot oil, I have given instructions wherever necessary for lowering the heat if you have gas rings or for removing the pan from the heat for a moment or two if your rings are electric and take time to cool: this is to make quite sure that the spices do not burn. If they do, they will give the dish a singularly unpleasant, bitter taste which cannot be remedied: you will have to start again. I only mention this here to give it emphasis: if you follow the directions in the recipes, it will not happen.

STIR-FRYING

This is a method of cooking in which ingredients are cut up very small, fried at high (or sometimes medium) heat and stirred continuously to prevent burning. The small size of the pieces into which they are chopped means that cooking is very rapid: this not only saves fuel but also preserves their crispness and flavour to a remarkable degree (their small size also explains the use of chopsticks). As size affects cooking time, I have given details throughout; in addition I have given the exact time for which each item should fry before the next is added. However, these times should be regarded merely as guides. Cooking times are influenced not only by size but also by the age and condition of ingredients, the heat of the oil and, in particular, the amount of food already in the pan: the items added last, when the pan is fairly full, will cook relatively slowly. There is also the question of taste: some people like vegetables (or beef) cooked more thoroughly than others. The chief purpose of the table on page 192, which I have included for those who want to compose their own dishes, is to give the order in which to add items (although even this is not invariable).

To my mind there are only two drawbacks to stir-frying: one, which I have already mentioned, is the amount of oil needed; the other is that ingredients with different times have to be kept separate before cooking, which takes up space and plates. One way of overcoming this is to pile them in tiers on the same plate with the item to be added last at the bottom and the one which takes longest to cook at the top. The tiers are separated by double layers of kitchen paper, which serve the added purpose of ensuring that they are dry: when the time comes to add them to the pan, the paper can be used as a funnel. I have not suggested this method with the recipes because of its extravagance with paper; however, you may find it useful on occasion

• BASIC PREPARATIONS • AND ACCOMPANIMENTS

In the first part of this chapter, I have given instructions for making a few basic items that are needed as ingredients for the recipes. All except fresh (as opposed to tinned or powdered) coconut milk and unsalted or only slightly salted chicken or vegetable stock can be bought ready-prepared from Oriental stores or the large supermarket chains, but can be made easily and more cheaply at home. The three items which are called for most often are the coconut milk, the stock and the ghee or clarified butter. Stock and ghee can be simmered whenever it is convenient and kept until required; coconut milk, however, must be used within 24 hours.

In the second half of the chapter, several versions of raita, a mild, flavoured yoghurt, are included. These are intended primarily to go with Indian-style dishes but are also excellent in their own right as a healthier alternative to fruit yoghurt. Similarly, I recommend Tomato Chutney with Red-Pepper not only as an accompaniment to Indian dishes but also to add interest to sandwiches or to serve with cheese. Raita cannot be kept for more than an hour or so. However, chutney, like stock and ghee, can be made whenever you have the time and, if stored in a sterilized, screw-top jar, will last for up to a year.

• GHEE •

Just as clarified animal fats were used in Britain before cheap, agreeable cooking-oils became available, so ghee, the equivalent of clarified butter, is traditional in India. Ordinary butter tends to brown when used for cooking because it consists of not only fat but a substantial proportion (20 per cent) of lactose and milk solids, plus water (which causes spitting); however, when purified it can be heated to a high temperature without burning. The rich taste of ghee transforms certain dishes, notably those made with vegetables or dairy products – namely, eggs, yoghurt and paneer; its chief disadvantage is that it is expensive. For this reason (rather than its cholesterol content) I have recommended using it relatively sparingly and often suggested combining it with oil, which gives its flavour at lesser cost.

Like other preparations such as garam masala, it can be bought ready-prepared (some supermarkets sell it), but it is very easy to make yourself. All that is involved is keeping the butter heated at a low temperature until the water it contains has evaporated and the solid impurities have separated out so that they can be strained off, leaving pure fat. The only difficulty you may have is in keeping the temperature of the butter sufficiently low: if it becomes hot enough to simmer for any length of time, it will brown in the same way as in cooking.

When made and cold, the ghee will solidify to some extent but, unlike butter, will remain grainy. It will keep for 6 weeks if stored somewhere cool or for several months in the refrigerator.

You will need a new disposable cleaning-cloth for straining it and a covered pot or carton for storage (you could use an empty margarine or ice-cream container) but make sure that it is perfectly clean.

Makes 190 g/6 oz

• INGREDIENTS •

250 g/8 oz butter, preferably
unsalted or only lightly salted

Smallish saucepan
New disposable cleaning-cloth
Covered pot or carton (for storage)

• METHOD •

1 Put the butter into the saucepan and set over very low heat until it has melted: watch it to ensure that it does not bubble. Turn down the heat even lower (probably as low as possible) so that the surface of the fat remains undisturbed and leave for 40–45 minutes. A sediment, which if it does not bubble and brown will be white, will form on the top and a streaky layer of milk solids will collect at the bottom.
2 Allow to cool a little. Strain through the cloth into a bowl and pour into the pot or carton. Leave to become cold and cover. Assuming that the butter did not burn, the ghee when cold and solidified will be a clear, bright yellow. (The cloth can be washed and used as normal.)

• GARAM MASALA •

'Masala' means spice mixture and 'garam' hot – which is slightly confusing, since the whole point of the masala is that it contributes aroma and flavour rather than heat. Unlike curry flavourings, it is not used normally at the beginning of cooking, so that it permeates the dish, but at or near the end. Prepared powders can be bought from Indian stores or health-food shops but these will not have the freshness and taste of those made at home. Every cook has his or her own variation or variations: some versions are gentle and fragrant, others more piquant. I have already given one recipe elsewhere (based on Jill Norman's, from *The Complete Book of Spices*): the following is similar but has a little more bite.

The spices can be toasted in a thick pan over a ring or baked in the oven, which is dearer (unless you are using the oven anyway) but gives a more even result and, in crisping them more effectively, makes them easier to crush. With either method, as when you use spices directly for cooking, it is important to avoid burning them. Another point to bear in mind is that the toasted or baked spices will smell fairly strong, so unless you have an efficient extractor fan, open the window or door.

If stored in an airtight jar or carton (a freezer container with a fitted lid is ideal), the masala will stay fresh for several months, although it will gradually become less potent.

Makes about 20 teaspoons

• INGREDIENTS •

7.5-cm/3-inch stick cinnamon	*3 teaspoons black peppercorns*
2 bayleaves	*2½ teaspoons cardamom pods*
3 teaspoons cumin seeds	*2 teaspoons cloves*
1 tablespoon plus 1 teaspoon coriander seeds	*1 teaspoon mace*

Thick-based saucepan or baking tray

• METHOD •
TO TOAST IN A SAUCEPAN

1 Put the cinnamon stick, bayleaves and cumin into the saucepan and toast over medium heat, shaking constantly, for 1–2 minutes or until the cumin is just starting to darken. Tip immediately into a mortar (the spices will continue to cook if left in the hot saucepan).

2 Toast the coriander, peppercorns, cardamom pods and cloves for 1–3 minutes or until just starting to change colour. Tip at once into the mortar.

3 Allow to cool a little. Add the mace and crush the spices to a fine powder. This takes me a good 20 minutes; however, as you are younger and more energetic, you may be able to do it much more quickly. Check that the masala is completely cold and store in an airtight container.

TO BAKE IN THE OVEN

Pre-heat the oven to 200°C/400°F/Gas Mark 6. Line the baking-tray with cooking-foil. Spread out the coriander seeds, peppercorns, cardamoms and cloves and bake for 2 minutes. Add the bayleaves, cinnamon and cumin and bake for 3–4 minutes more or until the spices have just begun to darken. Remove from the oven, allow to cool a little, then tip into a mortar. Add the mace and crush as above.

• TO BREAK AND • PREPARE FRESH COCONUTS

In times past, uninhibited by good advice, members of my family thoroughly enjoyed breaking coconuts: having pierced the eyes and drunk the water, they either threw them downstairs or dropped them onto the terrace from their bedroom windows. As the nuts were, of course, shattered into small pieces, the wastage was enormous. All this has been ended by Pat Chapman (of the Curry Club), who recommends baking in the oven before breaking: if it does not actually save time, this halves the preparation work and reduces wastage to almost nil.

Check that the coconut contains water (see page 10).

• INGREDIENTS •

1 *coconut*

Sharp knife
Grater

• METHOD •

1 Pre-heat the oven to 200°C/400°F/Gas Mark 6. Pierce the eyes at the top of the nut with a nail, screwdriver or awl, and drain off the water (which is sweet but not the coconut milk referred to in recipes). Hit the nut around the middle with a hammer or pestle to encourage it to break into even halves and bake for 15 minutes. The heat causes the shell to shrink and crack: it will either fall off without further interference or can be prised easily from the meat with a knife.

2 Peel the brown skin from the flesh with the sharp knife. As fragments of skin will inevitably stick to the flesh, wash it thoroughly in cold water.

3 For the recipes in this book, you will need grated coconut. Cut the nut into quarters or similar-sized chunks and grate finely: since you cannot avoid wasting the end of each piece as you grate, there is no need to cut the nut into too many pieces. Without too much wastage, a nut will give 250–280 g/8–9 oz meat.

• COCONUT MILK •

To make milk from grated fresh or desiccated coconut, put 250 g/8 oz of the nut into a bowl and add 600 ml/1 pint very hot but not boiling water for fresh or just-boiled (that is, almost boiling) water for desiccated. Stir and leave for 20–25 minutes. Turn into a sieve and press out as much liquid as you can using the back of a tablespoon. Discard the flesh. You should be left with about 450 ml/¾ pint milk. Allow to become cold and store, covered, in the refrigerator. After a few hours the milk will separate into fat and water: stir before use. Do not keep for more than 24 hours.

• STOCK •

I know that to many readers making stock seems boring and unnecessary; however, stock plays a central role in Far-Eastern (although not Indian) cookery, since it is used not only for soups and similar dishes but also for the sauces that accompany stir-fried items. Whenever practicable, I have incorporated making it into the recipe: the chicken and vegetable stocks given below will cover all the other instances where it is needed in this book. I do not recommend stock cubes if only because they are usually salty, and so are the sauces (for example, soy) with which stir-fried dishes are flavoured. In the absence of home-made stock, water is usually a better alternative.

As sauces for stir-fried dishes call for only a little stock at a time, I suggest making a sensible amount and freezing it in the compartments of an ice-cube tray. Small quantities can then be defrosted as needed. If you want the tray for ice, the cubes can be transferred when solid into a foodbag.

I should emphasize that making stock in the way described below is not expensive. Chicken stock, in effect, costs nothing, since you can eat the chicken (the only other ingredient needed is a pinch of salt); the vegetables used for vegetable stock will have to be thrown away, but consist of only a carrot, an onion and two outside sticks of celery.

• CHICKEN STOCK •

To obtain a really rich, strong flavour you need a whole carcase, such as you will have if you buy a chicken for Red-baked Chicken with Shiitake Mushrooms (page 155); alternatively, butchers will sometimes give you a carcase for nothing. However, a pair of free-range chicken legs will yield a very reasonable broth: use the meat for fried rice (page 113) or chicken salad (page 138), served if possible on the same day, since the simmered chicken tends to become dry if it is kept.

It is important to use a free-range rather than a battery-reared chicken, not only for ethical reasons but also because it has larger bones and far more flavour.

Makes 750–900 ml/1¼–1½ pints, or 375 ml/13 fl oz if reduced

• INGREDIENTS •

2 *chicken legs*

Salt

Saucepan with a lid

• METHOD •

1 Skin the legs: pull the skin sharply from the thickest corner. If you cannot separate it from the bone at the end, use a knife or scissors. Wash the legs thoroughly in cold water and put into the saucepan with a lid. Wash your hands and the knife or scissors (as a health precaution it is advisable to wash utensils

and your hands promptly after contact with raw meat, particularly poultry). Add a small pinch of salt and 1.1 litres/ 2 pints water or as much more as you need to cover the chicken. Bring to the boil, skim and add a little cold water; return to the boil and, if necessary, skim again. Cover and simmer gently for 45–50 minutes until the meat is very tender, no pink liquid emerges when it is pierced in the thickest part and you can cut it easily from the bones with a blunt knife. Remove from the pan, leaving the cooking liquid.

2 When the legs are cool enough to handle, cut off the meat: reserve this for another dish. Return the bones, plus the gristle to the pan. Bring back to the boil, cover and simmer for another 2–3 hours. Strain, throw away the bones, cover with a plate and leave to cool.

3 As the chicken was skinned before starting, the broth will not be very fatty (most of the fat on chicken is removed with the skin). If you need stock straight away, it is ready for use. However, for freezing it should be skimmed of fat thoroughly: chill it in the refrigerator for a few hours and remove any fat which solidifies on the surface. You can freeze it as it is if you have more than one ice-tray or a carton large enough to hold it (but note that if it is frozen in one vessel, you will have to defrost it all at once). Otherwise, return it to the saucepan and reduce by boiling briskly until only 375 ml/13 fl oz are left: this will just fill a 12-compartment tray. Allow to become cold, pour into the tray, cover with foodwrap and freeze. Depending on the temperature of the kitchen, the cubes will take 2–3 hours to defrost.

Unfrozen, the stock will keep for 3 days in the refrigerator; you can then boil it briskly for 10–12 minutes and keep it for a further 2 days.

• VEGETABLE STOCK •

Vegetable stock is a quicker option than chicken in that it takes only 20–25 minutes to simmer and does not need chilling and skimming. Unfrozen, however, it should not be kept for more than 24 hours.

Makes about 375 ml/13 fl oz

• INGREDIENTS •

2 outside sticks celery   *1 medium onion*

1 largish carrot

Saucepan with a lid

• METHOD •

1 Cut the leaves from the celery, then wash and slice moderately finely. Peel and finely slice the carrot. Peel and chop the onion. Put all the vegetables into the saucepan with 600 ml/1 pint water. Bring to the boil, cover and simmer gently for 20–25 minutes. Strain through a sieve, pressing out as much liquid as possible with the back of a spoon; throw away the vegetables. Cover and leave to become cold. Either use fresh or freeze as above.

• ONION CHIPS •

These are simply pieces of onion dried in the oven and then fried brown so that they are very crisp: rather like slices of garlic fried brown, they add a final touch to dishes which, in particular, might otherwise lack textural interest. You can buy them ready-prepared, but they are extremely easy to make at home. If stored in the refrigerator, they will keep for at least 10 days.

Makes 6-8 servings

• INGREDIENTS •

250 g/8 oz (2 smallish or 1 large) onion

1½ tablespoons or 40 g/1½ oz ghee

Baking-tray
Wok or frying-pan

• METHOD •

1 Pre-heat the oven to 100°C/200°F/Gas Mark ¼ and line the baking-tray with cooking-foil. Peel the onion(s) and chop into pieces about 5 mm/less than ¼ inch wide and 7 mm–1 cm/⅓–½ inch long. Spread over the baking-tray and dry in the oven for 35–40 minutes.

2 Line a large plate with a double layer of kitchen paper. Melt the ghee over medium heat in the wok and fry the dried onion pieces for 5–6 minutes or until an even mid-brown, turning constantly (a wok is better for frying them than a frying-pan because if any of the chips colour too quickly you can prevent them from cooking further by pushing them up the sides of the pan). Remove from the heat but keep on turning for a moment or two while the oil cools. Transfer to the paper-lined plate to drain off surplus oil. When quite cold, put into a covered pot or jar and store in the refrigerator.

• RAITA WITH CUCUMBER •

Raita is flavoured yoghurt which is served with Indian meals to add a cool element to dishes in much the same way as chutney adds zest. Cucumber has a similarly cooling effect.

For 3–4

• INGREDIENTS •

½ medium-sized cucumber	1 mild green chilli
Salt, some of which should be finely ground	About 1 teaspoon sugar
½ small lemon	250 g/8 oz plain whole-milk yoghurt (preferably mild)
2 spring onions	

Grater

• METHOD •

1 Peel and coarsely grate the cucumber (I suggest peeling it because the skin is tougher than the flesh and difficult to grate evenly). Sprinkle with fine salt and leave to sweat in a sieve or colander for 30 minutes. Rinse under the cold tap and transfer to a plate lined with kitchen paper to drain.

2 Squeeze the ½ lemon. Cut the roots and green leaves from the onions; peel off and discard the outer layer and slippery underskin, and chop into very fine rings. Wash and dry the chilli; trim the stalk end, slit, remove the seeds and inner pith and chop very finely. Do not rub your eyes while chopping it and wash your hands afterwards.

3 Stir the onions, chilli, cucumber and sugar into the yoghurt with 1 teaspoon salt and 4 teaspoons lemon juice. Taste: the exact amount of sugar needed varies according to the mildness of the yoghurt. Add just a little more if required. If you do not intend to serve the raita immediately, cover and store in the refrigerator: do not, however, keep for more than a few hours.

• RAITA WITH CUCUMBER • AND MINT

This is the same as the previous recipe except that mint is used instead of the chilli and onions.

You will need 2 spears of mint or enough for 2 tablespoons when chopped. Wash it, pull the leaves from the stems, blot dry with kitchen paper and chop finely.

• RAITA WITH CUMIN •

Proceed as for Raita with Cucumber, but substitute 1 teaspoon of finely crushed cumin for the lemon juice.

· TOMATO CHUTNEY WITH ·
RED PEPPPER

The pepper adds to the cost of this in terms of both money and preparation time, but it is more than worth it for the rich, sweet flavour it gives. The mixture smells fairly potently of vinegar as it cooks (open the window and avoid simmering it during a meal); the finished product, however, does not taste of it at all.

Although it is not totally essential, I strongly recommend peeling the pepper for this recipe: this is fairly quick if you have a gas ring but takes rather longer if you use the grill or oven (see below).

If you want the chutney to keep, you will have to sterilize the jar in which it is stored: you can then keep it like jam for up to a year.

Makes 500 g/1 lb

· INGREDIENTS ·

1 small red pepper

Oil

500 g/1 lb fairly ripe tomatoes

125–150 g/4–5 oz
(1 medium/2 small) onions

2 cloves garlic

1 moderately hot chilli (preferably red)

250 g/8 oz caster sugar

150 ml/¼ pint red-wine vinegar

Tongs or oven-cloth (for skinning the pepper) if your rings are gas or small baking-dish if your rings are electric
Foodbag or foodwrap
Sharp knife (for dicing the pepper)
Smallish saucepan
500 g/1 lb jar with a screw top
Saucepan deep enough to cover the jar
Baking-tray
2 oven-cloths or thick tea-towels

• METHOD •

1 The pepper must be charred before it can be skinned. The quickest and cheapest way to do this is over a gas burner; otherwise, you can use the oven or grill (if it is not needed for anything else, however, the oven in particular is an expensive option). If you have gas rings, turn the smallest to medium/low and place the pepper in the middle of the burner until the part in contact with the flames is black and blistered. Turn it with tongs or (after extinguishing the flame) with the aid of an oven glove or cloth: do not use a knife or fork, since if the pepper is pierced the sweet juices which collect inside will be lost. Repeat until the whole pepper is black. Allow to cool for a few moments, put it into the foodbag or wrap in foodwrap, seal and leave for 10–15 minutes. The burnt skin can now be peeled or rubbed off easily. Wipe any charred fragments from the flesh and put into a bowl. Cut off the top and discard the core and seeds; reserve the juice. Dice the flesh very finely.

Charring the pepper under the grill will take about 15 minutes. Set the grill to high, paint the pepper with oil, put it in the small baking-dish and grill for 5–6 minutes or until the top is black or well browned. Turn with tongs or an oven-glove and repeat until the whole pepper is browned. Put it into a foodbag or cover with foodwrap and continue as above.

In the oven, the pepper will take 30–40 minutes. Pre-heat the oven to 220°C/425°F/Gas Mark 7, paint the pepper with oil as before and roast until brown. Continue as above.

When the pepper is grilled or roasted, the skin comes away more readily than when it is charred over a flame, but the flesh will be cooked and slippery, which makes it harder to chop: use a sharp knife.

2 Skin the tomatoes: cover with boiling water, leave for 30 seconds, drain, and immerse in cold water; the skins will now peel off easily. Chop the tomatoes, discarding the hard cores. Peel and very finely chop the onion and garlic. Wash the chilli, trim the stalk end and dice the flesh as finely as possible, keeping the seeds. Do not rub your eyes while handling it and wash your hands afterwards.

3 Put all the prepared ingredients into the smallish saucepan with the sugar and vinegar and simmer for 1 hour or until the mixture is reduced and fairly thick, stirring at intervals. Then

cook for another 5 minutes, stirring constantly, until it is of the consistency of jam and slightly caramelized. (If you do not stir, it may burn at the bottom.) Remove from the heat.

4 While the mixture simmers, sterilize the jar. Wash both jar and top thoroughly with hot water and detergent, rinse well and put into the deep saucepan; the jar should be upright. Place a tablespoon inside the jar. Cover all but the top of the handle of the spoon with water, bring to the boil and boil briskly for 10 minutes. Pre-heat the oven to 150°C/300°F/Gas Mark 2; line the baking-tray with cooking-foil. Using a cloth (the handle may be hot) turn the jar upside-down on the spoon to drain out the water: then place on the baking-tray, still upside-down. Handle with the second cloth and take care not to touch the inside. Fish out the top with the sterilized spoon and place, the 'right' way up, next to the jar. Return the spoon to the saucepan. Dry the top and jar in the oven for 10–15 minutes or until there is no sign of moisture on the foil; remove from the oven but leave on the foil, without moving, until the chutney is ready. Use the sterilized spoon to fill the jar. Screw on the top and leave to become cold before storing somewhere cool.

• SHOBHNA'S GREEN-CHILLI • CHUTNEY

This is, or should be, decidedly hot, but it is sweet, refreshing and really tastes of coriander. It is not the preserved type of chutney: store for up to 7 days in a covered jar or pot in the refrigerator.

There is no point in making it with very mild chillies: cut a small piece from each and taste before starting.

Makes about 10 teaspoons

• INGREDIENTS •

Small bunch coriander (enough for 2 tablespoons when chopped)

1 small or ½ large lemon
4 large or 6 small green chillies

25 g/1 oz *unsalted peanuts*   1 *teaspoon sugar*

1 *teaspoon salt*

• METHOD •

1 Trim the ends of the coriander stalks, wash and blot dry with kitchen paper; chop finely. Squeeze the lemon. Wash and dry the chillies; trim the stalk ends and dice the flesh very finely, keeping the seeds. Do not touch your eyes while handling them and wash your hands directly afterwards. (It may seem unnecessary to dice the ingredients when the next step is to crush them to a paste, but it makes crushing very much easier.)
2 Crush the peanuts in a mortar. Add the chillies and coriander and pound to a smooth paste. Stir in the salt, sugar and 2 tablespoons lemon juice; mix thoroughly.

• VATCH'S CHARRED • CHILLI SAUCE

This is made with chillies plus tomatoes, garlic and shallots or onions, grilled until they are soft and slightly blackened. The charred taste is part of its attraction; it is also very hot – more so than you might perhaps expect from the ingredients – because grilling concentrates flavour. When I first made it I did not realize the extent to which this applies and generously coated a piece of chop with it: the result sent me leaping across the room. You do not need more than a scraping per mouthful.

The recipe on which this is based comes from Vatcharin Bhumichitr's *The Taste of Thailand* (Pavilion), where it is given as an accompaniment to steamed fish. It goes with fish particularly well (see Grilled Fish with Garlic and Mushrooms on page 101) but can also be used to enliven any number of other fairly plain dishes, such as grilled or baked chicken, pork or lamb chops and tofu with raw or cooked vegetables.

A vegetarian version can be made by omitting fish sauce, increasing the amount of lemon juice to 1½ tablespoons, and adding 1 scant teaspoon salt. I also especially recommend vegetarians to use shallots rather than onion, since without fish sauce the taste of onion is too strong (shallots are milder).

It is vital to use reasonably potent chillies: before starting, test them by cutting a small piece from each and taking a cautious bite. If you cannot find fresh red ones, use green.

With the quantities given, you will need only about half the sauce for one meal: the rest can be stored (covered) for up to 4 days in the refrigerator.

Makes 8–10 teaspoons

• INGREDIENTS •

2 medium (not large) tomatoes

2 medium/large shallots or 1 medium onion

2 moderately hot fresh red chillies, preferably large

6 fair-sized cloves garlic

½ lemon

1½ tablespoons fish sauce

Grill-pan

• METHOD •

1 Peel the tomatoes (see page 31) and cut out the hard cores. Peel the shallots or onion; if using an onion cut it in half lengthways – that is, from root to stalk end. Wash the chillies but leave them whole. Remove only the papery outer skin of the garlic.

2 Heat the grill to medium and line the grill-pan with cooking-foil. Grill the chillies and garlic for 1½–2 minutes, turning at least once, until charred to a light brown but not black. Keep a careful eye on the chillies, since they tend to blacken quickly. Remove the chillies and garlic and replace them in the pan with the tomatoes and shallots/onion. Grill for 12 minutes, turning the shallots/onion several times: if either becomes very black, remove the outer layer.

3 While the shallots/onion and tomatoes grill, chop and crush the chillies and garlic. Leave until cool enough to handle. Peel the garlic: if the flesh underneath the skin is a little browned, so much the better. Chop fairly finely. Cut off the stalks of the chillies and chop finely: do not rub your eyes while handling

them and wash your hands afterwards. Put both garlic and chillies, including the seeds of the chillies, into a mortar and crush to a paste. (It may seem superfluous to chop them before crushing, but it makes crushing very much easier.)

4 Leave the tomatoes and shallots/onion to cool. Chop the shallots/onion (which will be soft and slippery); add to the mortar and crush thoroughly. Chop the tomatoes; add and crush little by little. (I suggest adding them little by little because they will make the paste increasingly moist and crushing progressively more difficult: by the time both are incorporated, you will be mixing rather than crushing).

5 Squeeze and add 2 teaspoons lemon juice (or 1½ tablespoons for the vegetarian version); add and thoroughly stir in the fish sauce (or 1 scant teaspoon salt). The sauce will now be about as thick as jam. Serve cold.

• RED-CHILLI OIL •

This is simply chilli-impregnated oil used to add heat to Chinese-style dishes. It can be bought but is easy to make yourself. You can use fresh or dried chillies or chilli powder: whereas for most purposes I favour fresh chillies, in this instance I recommend dried or powdered. The dried chillies can be whole or crumbled – crumbled ones save time. If you use powder, make sure that it is labelled as hot.

The oil is potent, so you will need only a few drops.

Makes about 150 ml/¼ pint

• INGREDIENTS •

6 dried red chillies (enough for 4 scant teaspoons when roughly diced) or 4 scant teaspoons crumbled chillies or 2 teaspoons hot chilli powder

150 ml/¼ pint groundnut oil

4–5 cubes of stale bread (for testing the temperature of the oil)

Small, thick-based saucepan large enough to cover your ring
New disposable cleaning-cloth (if available)

• METHOD •

1 If using whole chillies, roughly dice them.

2 Check that the saucepan is perfectly dry: pour in the oil and set over high heat for 3 minutes. Place the handle towards the back to reduce the risk of accidents. Gently lower a bread cube into the oil. When it turns gold in the time it takes to count 40 (that is, in 40 seconds, which means that the oil has reached about 190°C/375°F), turn off the heat and immediately add the chilli: stand back in case it splutters. Leave for 30 minutes–1 hour or until cold. Strain through a disposable cleaning cloth if available; otherwise, you can use a sieve lined with kitchen paper. As the oil will not filter readily through the paper, however, this will take a little time. A few dark specks of chilli may remain in it, but these do not matter since it is used for sprinkling at table rather than cooking. Store in a cool place in a stoppered bottle.

   If thoroughly washed, the cloth can be used for cleaning in the usual way.

. RICE .

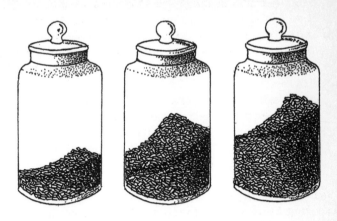

According to the latest archeological evidence, rice was cultivated in China before 6000 BC; in India and Pakistan remains have been found dating from before 2000 BC. Later it travelled to Japan and the Middle East; by the 13th century, it had reached Britain (*The Rice Book*, Sri and Roger Owen, Doubleday 1993). By the 18th century, rice puddings, generously enriched with eggs and cream and flavoured with cinnamon, sherry or orange-flower water, were firmly established in this country.

There are a number of main types of rice, which are distinguished by length and shape of grain, and many varieties within the types. In general the longer the grain, the harder and nuttier the texture: the longest-grained type is Basmati, which comes from north India and Pakistan and is especially suitable for curries. The shortest-grained type is pudding rice: another sort with short-grain characteristics, although the grain is in fact quite long, is glutinous or 'sticky' rice, which, as the name suggests, becomes gluey or sticky when cooked. A fairly soft, medium-grained type which I especially recommend for Far-Eastern-style dishes is Thai fragrant (sometimes known as 'jasmine') rice; a short-grained type but not so short-grained as pudding rice is Italian rice, which is used for risottos. Besides the different types, rice is processed in various ways: you can buy it brown or white, parboiled (which is white rice fortified with some of the nutrients of the husk), pre- or part-cooked, and flaked or ground. In all the recipes that follow I have assumed you will use it raw.

The usual way of cooking rice for savoury dishes is to simmer it until just tender in a certain amount of water; sometimes it is coated with oil first, or it may be stir-fried afterwards. Brief directions are given with all the recipes, but I have described the basic method here in more detail.

• PLAIN SIMMERED RICE •

Different cooks may use different methods of cooking plain rice. For instance, some use special steamers and some, including Shobhna Shah, soak the rice before cooking it, which softens the grains. I have not adopted this option here, although I have recommended it for puddings and other dishes, because it means waiting before starting to cook.

To make plain rice, start by weighing it, then rinse in a sieve under the cold tap until the water which runs from it is clear or almost clear – this removes surplus starch. Turn the rice into a medium-sized saucepan with a lid and add 810 ml/1⅓ pints water for 450 g/14 oz (4 servings), 600 ml/1 pint for 310 g/10 oz (3–4 servings), or in the same proportion – that is, approximately twice the volume of water to weight; for brown rice, add a dessertspoonful extra. If you have no scales, deduce the weight from the packet or use a mug (a full 300-ml/½-pint mug = 250 g/8 oz). Absolute precision is not essential, since if there is slightly too much water, it will evaporate while the rice stands after cooking; if there is not quite enough liquid the rice will form a gold or brownish crust at the bottom of the saucepan which many people (myself included) consider the best part of it: it can be kept and used, but so far as I am concerned it is the cook's perquisite. However, do not be tempted to add too little water deliberately because rice varies in absorbency and unless the shortage is only very slight, it will not cook properly.

If you like, add salt. Those who eat rice habitually almost always cook it without because salt interferes with its natural flavour, but if you are used to it you may prefer a little. Given the saltiness of soy and fish sauce and the spiciness of Indian dishes, however, you will not need much: just add a pinch.

Bring the water to the boil, stir thoroughly, reduce the heat to a very gentle simmer and cover: the water should only just move under the lid. Cook for 10–12 minutes for Thai rice, 18 minutes for white Basmati, 20 minutes for other types of white rice, or 30 minutes for brown rice. Leave to rest, covered, for at least 10 minutes: this is important because it gives the rice time to dry and become separate-grained. If you like, you can leave it longer: kept covered on a warm cooker, it will stay hot for 20 minutes or longer.

If you succeed in achieving a brown crust but find that some of the rice has stuck to the saucepan, do not try to scrape it off but leave the pan to soak. It will then come away easily.

• SPICED RICE •

Whereas hot and other strongly flavoured accompaniments need the blandness of plain rice as a contrast, milder Indian-style dishes are often given additional interest with rice flavoured with spices. How many spices you use and in what quantity depends on personal preference and on the dish: the minimum, which Shobhna sometimes serves and which gives a subtle, slightly sweet background taste, is a small piece of cinnamon and two cloves. However, for the recipes in which I have suggested it in this book I favour a stronger version, which is similar to Pat Chapman's in 250 *Favourite Curries* (Piatkus).

This dish is quick to prepare: except for opening the cardamom pods, none of the spices need crushing. The rice thus takes very little more time than plain simmered rice takes to cook.

The main effect of the turmeric is to colour the rice yellow: omit it by all means.

For 3–4

• INGREDIENTS •

310 g/10 oz white Basmati, Patna
or American long-grain rice

6 cardamom pods

1 tablespoon ghee or oil

6 cloves

5-cm/2-inch stick cinnamon

1 teaspoon fennel seeds

⅓ teaspoon cumin seeds

⅓ teaspoon salt (optional)

½ teaspoon ground turmeric
(optional)

Saucepan with a lid

• METHOD •

1 Rinse the rice under the cold tap until the water runs clear and leave to drain. Bruise the cardamoms in a mortar so that the pods are open (the seeds can be left intact).

2 Warm the ghee or oil over medium heat in the saucepan with a lid. Add the cardamoms and all the other spices (whole) and leave to fry for 40 seconds–1 minute or until the cumin pops. Add the rice and stir-fry until every grain is coated with oil. Pour in 600 ml/1 pint water, bring to the boil and stir. Cover and simmer for 18 minutes for Basmati or 20 minutes for other types of rice. Leave to stand, covered, for at least 10 minutes before serving.

• SHOBHNA'S SPINACH RICE •

This is wonderfully fresh tasting and, in contrast to Spiced Rice, contains no spices at all. Instead it is flavoured with vegetables, lemon and fresh coriander, with a hint of coconut and a generous infusion of chillies. Even the coriander is not essential: if you do not have any, use parsley. As it stands, the recipe includes six chillies, which give a pretty hot result, but those who prefer to can omit the two with the spinach and/or use three instead of four in the coconut and coriander paste.

Use fresh, real spinach. Sometimes beet spinach, which has larger leaves and thick white stems, is sold instead, but although it is an acceptable substitute for some purposes, it is unsuitable here (when fried, the leaves tend to disintegrate). Spinach on the root is usually in better condition than spinach picked by the leaf; baby spinach leaves save time because they will not need chopping but may be expensive.

For 3–4

• INGREDIENTS •

280 g/9 oz white Basmati rice

Salt

190 g/6 oz spinach

250 g/8 oz unpodded fresh or 125 g/4 oz frozen peas

Bunch fresh coriander or, if unobtainable, parsley (enough for 3 tablespoons when chopped)

25 g/1 oz fresh or desiccated coconut

½ small lemon

6 green chillies

½ teaspoon sugar

150–190 g/5–6 oz (1 medium) onion

1 tablespoon ghee

Saucepan with a lid (for the rice)
Grater (if using fresh coconut)
Wok or frying-pan
Soufflé or other ovenproof dish about 20 cm/8 inches in diameter and 7.5 cm/3 inches deep

• METHOD •

1 Rinse the rice until the water runs clear and put into the saucepan with a lid. Add 570 ml/19 fl oz salted or unsalted water and bring to the boil. Stir, cover and simmer for 18 minutes. Leave to rest, covered, until the other ingredients are prepared (see Step 5).

2 Pick over the spinach, removing roots, weeds and damaged or rotten leaves. Wash, twice if necessary, and cut into strips 2.5cm/1 inch wide. (This is a chore: baby spinach leaves can be left whole.) Put on a plate lined with kitchen paper to dry.

3 Pod the peas if necessary. Just cover with slightly salted water and boil frozen ones for 2 minutes or fresh ones for 5–15 minutes or until tender (the time they will take depends on their age). Drain; keep covered if possible.

4 Trim the ends of the coriander stems; wash the coriander, blot dry with kitchen paper and chop finely. Coarsely grate the coconut if necessary. Squeeze the ½ lemon. Wash the chillies; trim the stalk ends, slit, remove the inner membrane and all or some of the seeds, and dice the flesh as finely as possible. Do not touch your eyes while chopping them and wash your hands immediately afterwards. Put the coriander, coconut and two-thirds of the chillies into a mortar with the sugar and 1 teaspoon salt. Pound to a rough paste, or at least enough to crush the chillies and coriander and release the juices. Stir in 1 tablespoon lemon juice and, if the coconut is desiccated, 1 tablespoon water.

5 Peel and finely slice the onion. Pre-heat the oven to 190°C/375°F/Gas Mark 5. Loosen the cooked rice with a fork; check that the spinach is dry and blot if necessary. Warm the ghee in the wok or frying-pan over medium heat and fry the onion for 3–4 minutes or until soft but not brown. Add the remaining third of the chillies and the spinach. Sprinkle with a very little salt and stir-fry for 1½–2 minutes or until the spinach is reduced in volume and has collapsed. Add the chilli and coriander paste and stir-fry for just long enough to mix it in thoroughly. Add the rice and peas and stir-fry for another 2 minutes. Remove from the heat.

6 Lightly butter the oven-proof dish. Turn the rice mixture into it; press it down, flatten the surface and cover with cooking-foil. Bake in the oven for 10–15 minutes; serve at once.

• FRIED RICE WITH •
BEANS AND RED PEPPER

This is an effective combination which in terms of taste needs nothing else. However, as it contains no high-protein ingredient, it has to be counted as an accompanying dish.

The rice must be set to simmer an hour or more before frying if it is to be light and dry: if fried while still wet, it will be sticky and heavy.

For 3–4

• INGREDIENTS •

310 g/10 oz Thai fragrant or white Patna or American long-grain rice

Salt

50 g/2 oz Kenya or other fine, stringless, green beans

1 large red pepper

90 g/3 oz button mushrooms

2 medium-sized sticks celery

125 g/4 oz (1 small to medium) onion

2 cloves garlic

2 tablespoons oil

2 tablespoons light soy sauce

Saucepan with a lid (for the rice)
Large wok or frying-pan
Wok-scoop or spatula (if available)

• METHOD •

1 Rinse the rice under the cold tap until the water runs clear. Put into the saucepan with a lid, add 600 ml/1 pint water, with or without salt, and bring to the boil. Stir, cover and simmer for 12 minutes for Thai or 20 minutes for other types of rice. Leave to rest, covered, for at least 45 minutes.

2 Top and tail and wash the beans; chop into 2-cm/¾-inch lengths and leave to dry on a plate lined with kitchen paper. Wash, dry and quarter the pepper; remove the core, seeds and white inner pith and dice into pieces about the size of peas. Trim the mushroom stalks; wash, dry and finely slice the mushrooms. Cut off the leaves and trim the root ends of the celery, pare off any discoloured patches, wash, dry and chop into 2-cm/¾-inch slices; then cut into sticks 5-mm/less than ¼-inch wide. Peel and finely chop the onion; peel and thinly slice the garlic.

3 Loosen the rice with a fork so that it can be turned easily into the pan. Set all the prepared ingredients plus the soy sauce within easy reach of the cooker. Warm the oil in the wok or frying-pan over high heat, add the garlic and allow to fry for 30 seconds or until starting to change colour. Add the pepper and stir for 20–30 seconds; add the celery and stir; add the onion and stir; add the beans and stir for 30 seconds. Add the mushrooms and stir for 1 minute. Lower the heat to medium: if your ring is electric and does not respond quickly to a change of setting, cool the pan by removing it for a second or two. Add the rice and stir-fry for 2 minutes using a wok-scoop or spatula (if available). Add the soy sauce, stir until absorbed and serve.

• SHOBHNA'S SAFFRON •
RICE WITH ALMONDS

This is another version of Spiced Rice (see page 39) and can be made by the same method – that is, by adding the uncooked rice to the fried spices and simmering them together. However, Shobhna simmers the rice before adding the spices, which means using a little extra ghee (it really is important to use ghee for this recipe) but gives a very much more luxurious, rich-tasting result.

The saffron, nuts and ghee, plus Basmati rice, make this relatively expensive, but as the nuts are high in protein it is an especially suitable accompaniment to vegetable dishes, notably Braised Broccoli with Lemon and Coriander (see page 163). Basmati rice should be used, since its hard, firm texture and nutty flavour match the nuts: if you want to reduce the cost, substitute peanuts for the cashew nuts.

A small packet of saffron, of which you will need approximately one-third to a half, costs £1.50–£2.00. The saffron will not only colour the rice a soft yellow but will also give it a subtle scent and taste: to retain the flavour, add the saffron to the rice after, rather than before, cooking and leave it to infuse while the rice rests.

As no chopping or crushing is needed, except for bruising the cardamom pods, the dish is quick to prepare and entails very little work. Allowing 20 minutes for resting the rice, it will be ready to serve in under 45 minutes.

I have given quantities for only 310 g/10 oz rice because it is difficult to fry more in the usual-sized large wok.

For 3–4

• INGREDIENTS •

310 g/10 oz white Basmati rice

Salt

2 tablespoons milk

⅓–½ small packet saffron or 20–25 threads

2 tablespoons ghee

100 g/3½ oz unskinned whole almonds

100 g/3½ cashew nuts (for preference) or peanuts

6 cardamom pods

6 cloves

7.5-cm/3-inch stick cinnamon

Saucepan with a lid (for the rice)
Large wok or frying-pan
Fish-slice or perforated spoon

• METHOD •

1 Rinse the rice under the cold tap until the water runs clear. Put it into the saucepan with a lid, add 600 ml/1 pint water, and salt if you wish, and bring to the boil. Stir, lower the heat, cover and simmer for 18 minutes.

2 While the rice simmers, heat but do not boil the milk. Add the saffron and leave for a few minutes. Stir, so that the milk is coloured yellow. When the rice is cooked, stir in the saffron milk, with the red saffron threads: be thorough but gentle, taking care not to break the grains. Cover and leave to rest for 15–20 minutes.

3 Heat ½ tablespoon of the ghee in the wok or frying-pan over medium/low heat and add the nuts. Stir-fry for 1–2 minutes, until they are just beginning to brown (watch them carefully, since cashews especially burn easily). Remove at once from the heat and continue to stir for a moment or two, while the ghee cools. Transfer them to a plate with the fish-slice or perforated spoon, leaving the remains of the ghee in the pan.

4 When the rice has rested, loosen it with a fork. Bruise the cardamoms in a mortar, so that the pods are opened but the seeds intact. Add the rest of the ghee to the wok and warm over medium heat. Fry the cardamoms, cloves and cinnamon stick for 1 minute, turning often. Reduce the heat slightly, turn the rice into the pan and stir-fry just until all the grains are separate and coated with ghee. Add and stir in the nuts. Serve at once.

· SOUPS ·

In the East, the different dishes which make up a meal are not divided into courses as they are in the West, but served all at the same time. The only exceptions are small items which might be offered before the meal, in the same way as nuts or olives are here; fresh fruit, which would follow a Thai dinner; or thin soup or broth, which sometimes ends a meal in China – this is actually intended more as a drink than as food. The basic item on which Eastern meals are centred is starch – namely, rice, noodles or wheat products (not all noodles are made of wheat). Other dishes are served communally, with diners helping themselves in whatever order and quantity they wish. Like the different components of a conventional dinner in this country (and the meal overall), these dishes are planned to contrast in type, taste and texture. Thus, a crisp, stir- or deep-fried dish is complemented by a softer, more liquid one, which might be some sort of stew but could equally well be a soup. As rice already features on the menu, soups do not include it unless of the congee type, in which rice is simmered until it is almost disintegrating: congee, however, is typically a breakfast, rather than a main-meal, dish.

The soups in this chapter include Shehzad's Chicken with Lemon and Vegetable Broth, which is half-way to a stew in that the meat is not cut up but served on the bone; and Pork

Slivers and Mushrooms in Broth with Star Anise, which is the soup equivalent of a stir-fried dish. With some dishes, I have suggested serving the rice separately in the authentic, Oriental style, but in two, for the sake of simplicity, I have incorporated it into the soup. The last dish is a congee, which I have included partly to illustrate the versatility of rice (there is another, cheaper, one at the back of the book: see page 171).

Where the soup contains rice you should serve it promptly, since if it is left to stand the rice will continue to swell as it absorbs the liquid.

• LEMON AND LENTIL SOUP •

This is fairly hot and strongly infused with lemon: against it, the rice, which is served separately, tastes surprisingly nutty and sweet.

As you need only the lentils and lemon juice plus onions, chillies, spices and fresh coriander, it is remarkably cheap and contains nothing that you are likely to have to buy specially (except, perhaps, for the coriander).

The only drawback to the recipe is that you really do need to make stock: without it, the soup will be merely the sum of its parts. However, the spiced stock given below involves very little work (see Step 1) and takes only 25–35 minutes to simmer.

For 3–4

• INGREDIENTS •

STOCK

310 g/10 oz (2 medium) onions	8 cloves
3 cloves garlic	8 cardamom pods
2-cm/¾-inch piece fresh root ginger	7.5-cm/3-inch stick cinnamon
2 bayleaves	6 black peppercorns
2 teaspoons salt	

SOUP

1 medium to largish lemon	1 teaspoon yellow mustard seeds
100 g/3½ oz split red lentils	1 teaspoon black peppercorns
310 g/10 oz (1 large/2 medium) onions	310–400 g/10–13 oz white Patna or American long-grain rice
2.5-cm/1-inch piece fresh root ginger	Salt
2 green chillies	Small bunch coriander (enough for 2 tablespoons when chopped)
2 tablespoons ghee	
2 teaspoons coriander seeds	

Largish saucepan with a lid
Wok or large saucepan with a lid
Smaller saucepan with a lid (for the rice)

• METHOD •

1 First make the stock. Peel and quarter the onions and put them into the largish saucepan with a lid. Peel the garlic and ginger and roughly crush in a mortar. Add to the saucepan with the other ingredients (leave the spices whole). Pour in 1.8 litres/3 pints water and bring to the boil. Lower the heat, cover and simmer for 25–35 minutes.

2 Squeeze the lemon; pick over and rinse the lentils. Peel and finely chop the onions and ginger, rejecting any fibrous patches on the ginger: keep each separate. To chop onions quickly, cut in half lengthwise and place on the chopping-surface with the flat side downwards: then slice finely and cross-chop. Wash and dry the chillies and trim the stalk ends: unless you think that they are very hot, do not remove the seeds. Dice the flesh as finely as possible. Do not rub your eyes while chopping them and wash your hands directly afterwards.

3 Strain the stock, throwing away the solid ingredients. Warm the ghee in the wok or saucepan and fry the onions over medium heat for 3–4 minutes or until soft but not brown, turning often. Add the ginger and stir-fry for 30 seconds. Lower the heat: if your ring is electric and does not cool quickly, remove the pan for a moment or two. Add the chillies and turn in the oil; add the spices (whole) and stir-fry for 20–30 seconds. Add the lentils and stir. Pour in 1.5 litres/2½ pints of the stock, add 2 tablespoons of the lemon juice and bring to the boil. Stir thoroughly, boil moderately but not too briskly for 2 minutes, lower the heat and cover. Cook at a bare simmer for 40–50 minutes: the surface of the water should hardly move.

4 Start cooking the rice when the lentils have simmered for 10 minutes. Rinse in cold water until the water runs clear, put into the saucepan with a lid, and pour in 600 ml/1 pint water for 310 g/10 oz of rice or 800 ml/1⅓ pints for 400 g/13 oz. Add a little salt if you wish. Bring to the boil, stir, cover and simmer for 20 minutes. To ensure that it is really firm and dry and thus an effective textural contrast to the soup, be especially careful not to overcook it and leave to stand, covered, for at least 10 minutes.

5 Unless picked from your own plant, trim the ends of the coriander stems; wash, shake dry and chop finely. When the soup has simmered, add with 1 more tablespoon of the lemon juice. Taste, and add a little salt if necessary. Serve accompanied by the rice in a separate bowl.

• SHEHZAD'S CHICKEN •
WITH LEMON AND
VEGETABLE BROTH

Shehzad is a cookery writer from Hyderabad in south-east India (although her style of cookery is not specifically southern Indian). As a Muslim, she is forbidden to eat pork but unlike Jains, Buddhists and many Hindus, she is not a vegetarian. She has contributed a number of recipes to this book, of which some are moderately hot, but others delicately, rather than strongly, flavoured – as I particularly requested, since I wanted to show that Indian food is not necessarily heavily spiced but can be subtle, restrained and/or very simple. The only hint of heat in this soup comes from the black pepper, which is balanced by lemon; otherside the flavour depends almost entirely on the chicken.

Partly because the chicken is not chopped up but left on the bone, very little preparation is needed. The dish is also relatively low-calorie, since it contains no fat apart from a very small amount left on the chicken after skinning. Its fatlessness will be offset if you serve it with garlic bread, as Shehzad suggests: alternatively, accompany it with hot, plain crusty bread and Shobhna's Green-Chilli Chutney (page 32).

For 2

• INGREDIENTS •

1 scant teaspoon black peppercorns

4 coriander seeds

1 lemon

2 chicken legs

1 teaspoon salt

1 bayleaf

2 medium carrots

1 green pepper

50 g/2 oz white Patna or American long-grain rice

50 g/2 oz frozen sweetcorn or peas

• METHOD •

1 Crush the peppercorns and coriander seeds in a mortar; squeeze the lemon. Skin the chicken: pull the skin sharply from the thigh end. You may be able to pull it off over the bone at the bottom, but if this proves impossible, use a knife or scissors. Remove as much as you can of any fat remaining on the meat, wash thoroughly in cold water and put into a largish saucepan. Wash your hands and the utensils.

2 Add the crushed pepper and coriander seeds, 3 tablespoons lemon juice, the salt and the bayleaf to the chicken. Pour in 900 ml/1½ pints water, bring to the boil and skim. Lower the heat and cook, uncovered, at just above simmering (so that the water bubbles gently) for 20 minutes. Meanwhile peel and very finely slice the carrots; wash and quarter the pepper, discard the core, seeds and white inner pith and cut into fine strips.

3 When the chicken has been boiling for 20 minutes, rinse the rice and add with the carrot. Continue to boil for 10 minutes. Add the pepper and sweetcorn if you are using it and cook for another 10 minutes. Prod the chicken with a fork in the thickest part: if it is tender, no pink liquid appears when it is pierced to the bone and the flesh parts from the bone easily, it is ready. Add the peas if you are using them, boil gently for 2 minutes, and serve.

• PORK SLIVERS AND •
MUSHROOMS IN BROTH
WITH STAR ANISE

This is very much a main-course dish, and in China would be accompanied by other contrasting, probably stir- or deep-fried items. Serve it either as in the East, with individual bowls of rice and a separate dish of the soup to which you help yourselves, or pour it directly over the portions of rice.

Unsalted chicken stock is essential for this recipe. It is very easy to make (see page 25): you can use the chicken meat for another dish (see Fried Rice with Left-over Chicken and Prawns, page 113, or Left-over Chicken and Rice Salad, page 138).

Star anise is a black, star- or flower-shaped spice with a liquorice flavour. It is available from most supermarkets: if you cannot find it go to a good grocer or health-food shop.

Use pork loin chops, which have a large, solid area of lean meat, rather than chump or shoulder chops. As the fat is not needed, choose the leanest possible.

If necessary, the broth can be made several hours in advance (see Step 1).

For 3, or 4 at a pinch

• INGREDIENTS •

2 pork chops weighing
400–500 g/13 oz–1 lb
together

90 g/ 3oz button mushrooms

1 carrot

1 outside stick celery

3.5-cm/1⅓-inch piece fresh root
ginger

2 star anise

675 ml/1⅛ pints unsalted chicken
stock

4 tablespoons light soy sauce

3 tablespoons plus 1 teaspoon
medium-dry sherry

1 tablespoon dark soy sauce

1 teaspoon soft dark-brown sugar

Salt

Pepper

1 tablespoon oil

310–400 g/10–13 oz Thai fragrant,
Patna or American long-grain white
or brown rice

50 g/2 oz green cabbage, preferably
the inner part

50 g/2 oz Kenya or other fine,
stringless, green beans

3 cloves garlic

Large saucepan with a lid
Smaller saucepan with a lid (for the rice)

• METHOD •

1 Make the broth. Wash the chops in cold water and remove the bones and all the fat. Throw away the fat; put the bones into the large saucepan with a lid. Wash the mushrooms. Cut off the stems, trim and add to the saucepan; set the caps aside. Peel and slice the carrot and add to the pan. Trim the root ends, leaves and any brown streaks from the celery; wash, slice and add to the pan. Peel and slice 1.5 cm/⅗ inch of the ginger and add to the pan with the star anise. Pour in the stock, bring just to the boil, cover and simmer for 30–45 minutes or while you prepare the rest of the ingredients. Strain, throwing away the solid components, and add 3 tablespoons of the light soy sauce, 3 tablespoons of the sherry, the dark soy sauce and the sugar. If made in advance, cover and leave to cool.

2 Cut the pork into strips 5 mm/less than ¼ inch wide and 3 cm/1¼ inches long. Spread out on a plate and season very lightly with salt and more generously with pepper. Mix together the remaining tablespoon of light soy sauce, 1 teaspoon of the sherry and the oil. Pour over the pork and toss to mix. Leave the meat to marinate until needed.

3 Rinse the rice until the water runs clear and put into the smaller saucepan with a lid. Add 600 ml/1 pint salted or unsalted water for 310 g/10 oz or 800 ml/1⅓ pints for 400 g/13 oz. Bring to the boil, stir, cover and simmer for 12 minutes for Thai rice, 20 minutes for white Patna or American long-grain, or 30 minutes for brown. Leave to rest, covered, for 10 minutes.

4 Cut out any tough stalks from the cabbage, slice the leaves into strips the same size as the pork and wash. Top and tail the beans; wash and chop into 2-cm/¾-inch lengths. Finely slice the mushroom caps. Peel and thinly slice the garlic and the rest of the ginger.

5 When the rice has rested, bring the broth to the boil and adjust the heat so that it is boiling gently: that is, just bubbling. Add the ginger and garlic and cook for a few seconds. Add the beans and allow to return to the boil (the temperature of the broth will be lowered by the addition of cold items). Add the mushrooms and allow to return to the boil. If the broth seems much reduced, pour in 75–150 ml ⅛–¼ pint more water. Add the cabbage and pork with its marinade, bring back to the boil and cook for 1½ minutes or until the pork is white and opaque and the cabbage just tender. Serve the rice in individual bowls with the soup either poured over it or in a large separate bowl.

• CONGEE WITH SHIITAKE •
MUSHROOMS AND
BLACK-BEAN PASTE

Congee is, in effect, rice porridge: a little rice is simmered in a lot of stock for a long time so that the rice starch is released in the same way as with rice puddings. The low proportion of rice means that flavours are transmitted very clearly, so that it can be surprisingly delicious with relatively few ingredients.

However, lack of rice also means that, although it seems satisfying at the time, it is not very sustaining. The congee below is made with only 90 g/3 oz rice plus vegetable stock and the mushrooms, with no added fat (which makes it very suitable for anyone watching their weight): although oil and protein are added by the accompanying bean-paste sauce, you should serve it with plenty of bread.

Both the black-bean paste and the shiitake mushrooms are sold only at Oriental stores. The paste is made of fermented soya and black beans: do not be put off by its strong, salty smell. When added to chilli and crisp-fried garlic, it imparts a rich, distinctive tang to the congee and brings out the flavour of the mushrooms. It is not expensive: at the time of going to press, a 300-ml/½-pint jar costs about £1.60. The shiitake mushrooms, especially good-quality ones, are an extravagance but are widely used in Far-Eastern cookery. The smallest packets sold are 50 g/2 oz, of which you will need approximately half: use the other half for Red-baked Chicken with Shiitake Mushrooms (see page 155). I should point out, however, that you can buy the mushrooms more cheaply in larger quantities; the price also varies enormously according to quality (about £1.75–£3.75 for 50 g/2 oz). High-quality mushrooms have patterned caps (the cheaper ones are almost black) and a much stronger, clearer taste: in view of the cost, I cannot unreservedly recommend them – but try them just once if you can.

The vegetable stock can be made in advance, but once the rice is added, the congee should be served when it is ready, otherwise the rice will continue to absorb liquid and become increasingly mushy.

For 2–3

• INGREDIENTS •

25 g/1 oz dried shiitake mushrooms

3 outside sticks celery

190 g/6 oz (3 medium) carrots

150 g/5 oz (1 medium) onion

1 moderately hot green chilli

6 black peppercorns

90 g/3 oz Thai fragrant rice

1 teaspoon salt

2 large or 3 small cloves garlic

1.5-cm/⅗-inch piece fresh root ginger

1 moderately hot fresh or dried red chilli

1 tablespoon oil

2 tablespoons black-bean paste

Large saucepan
Small saucepan

• METHOD •

1 Cover the mushrooms with very hot (but not boiling) water and leave to soak for 25 minutes. Drain over a bowl to catch the liquor; slice fairly finely and pull off the stalks (which are tough). Set the mushroom caps aside and cover. Make up the liquor to 1.8 litres/3 pints with water.

2 Cut the leaves from the celery, then wash and slice fairly finely. Peel and slice the carrots. Peel and chop the onion. Wash the chilli and slit lengthways to expose the seeds (but leave them inside). Put the celery, carrots, onion, chilli, peppercorns and mushroom stalks into the large saucepan with the mushroom liquor and water, bring to the boil and simmer gently for 20–25 minutes. Strain, pressing as much liquid from the vegetables as possible with the back of a spoon; then throw them away.

3 Return the stock to the saucepan; rinse and add the rice. Bring to the boil, stir and simmer gently, uncovered, for 1 hour; stir fairly often, especially towards the end, since the rice tends to stick to the bottom of the pan. Provided that it is regularly stirred, however, a little sticking is not disastrous, since the slightly browned rice will add flavour to the congee.

4 Add the mushrooms and salt; stir and continue to simmer, stirring frequently, for 25–30 minutes. If the congee becomes very solid, add a little water.

5 Peel the garlic and ginger and dice finely, taking care to remove any fibrous patches on the ginger. Wash and dry the chilli and trim the stalk end; dice as finely as possible, keeping the seeds. Do not touch your eyes while preparing it and wash your hands directly afterwards. When the mushrooms have simmered for 25 minutes, warm the oil over medium heat in the small saucepan and fry the garlic and ginger until starting to change colour. Add the chilli and stir; add the bean paste and stir. Remove from the heat. Serve the congee with the bean-paste sauce separately.

· YOGHURT, CHEESE · AND TOFU DISHES

I have put yoghurt and cheese into the same chapter as tofu because, in effect, soya beans are the equivalent of milk in the Far East. In India, milk, yoghurt and fresh, soft cheese (paneer) are widely used in cooking; however, in China soya is favoured for economic reasons. Between them, soya products perform the same functions as dairy produce: beancurd or tofu has a similar consistency to cheese (though not the texture), while soy sauce and bean pastes provide flavour; in addition are soya milk and beancurd skins, which are dried sheets made of the residue thrown up as soya beans are simmered. Nutritionally, soy and dairy products are comparable, since soy is rich in protein and fermented items contain vitamin B12 (see Nutrition, page 189).

To highlight the similarities between tofu and cheese, I have given two parallel dishes in this chapter: deep-fried paneer balls which can be flavoured with either herbs or cumin, and deep-fried tofu balls which are flavoured with sherry and ginger. I have also given examples of how each can be used in cooking: other dishes containing tofu are Fried Rice with Aubergine and Tofu (page 71), Tofu Omelette (page 79), Crudités with Tofu and Charred Chilli Sauce (page 133) and Red-baked Beef with Tofu and Mushrooms, which is in the dinner-party chapter (page 153).

• PANEER •

In India, as elsewhere, vegetarians are forbidden to eat cheeses made in the traditional way with calves' rennet; nor is the climate favourable to the hard, European-type of cheese that has to be matured at a relatively low temperature (typically 13°C/55°F). However, fresh cheese curdled with lemon juice is very popular in India, both for cooking (as in Italy) and *per se*. If you want to eat it on its own you may like to flavour and/or deep-fry it (see page 62), or you can use it in sauces such as Shobhna's Paneer and Tomato Sauce (page 64) or for pullao (page 65).

Usually the cheese is made simply with milk and lemon juice; however, the cookery demonstrator Kumud Shah adds yoghurt, which makes it moister and more cohesive: hence her recipe for deep-fried paneer balls. Either way, it takes less than 10 minutes to make plus 20–30 minutes to drain; if you want to turn it into a relatively solid cheese, you will have to compress it for a further 3–4 hours.

Although you can use skimmed or semi-skimmed milk, I do not recommend it because it yields less paneer: 1.1 litres/ 2 pints skimmed milk will make only about 175 g/5½ oz.

Makes about 225 g/7 oz

• INGREDIENTS •

Either ½ large or 1 small lemon (2 tablespoons lemon juice)

or ½ small lemon (1 tablespoon juice) plus 2 generous tablespoons whole-milk yoghurt

1.1 litres/2 pints whole milk

⅓ teaspoon salt

Pinch of hot chilli powder

New disposable cleaning-cloth if available (failing this, you can use kitchen paper)

• METHOD •

1 Squeeze the lemon. Heat the milk until it is nearly boiling; then turn down the heat so that it will not boil over. As soon as

it starts to bubble and rise, add either 2 tablespoons lemon juice or 1 tablespoon lemon juice and the yoghurt. Stir vigorously, adjust the heat to a simmer and leave over the heat until you can see that the milk has curdled: this is more obvious with yoghurt than only lemon juice, since the yoghurt causes the lumps of curd to be quite large, whereas with lemon they may be small, like beads. Remove the pan from the heat and strain through a sieve lined with the cleaning-cloth or, if you have no cloth, kitchen paper. If you use kitchen paper, you may have to shake or tip the sieve to encourage the liquid to filter through. When all or most of it has drained away, rinse the curds under the cold tap to remove the traces of lemon. Leave the cheese to drain again for 20–30 minutes.

2 Mash the salt and chilli powder into the curds with a fork. For Paneer Pullao you can leave the cheese as it is; for paneer and tomato sauce, it should be pressed into a cohesive block. To press it, smooth it into an even layer about 1 cm/½ inch thick on a plate or large saucer, cover with the cloth or a double layer of kitchen paper and place a saucepan of water or some other heavy item on top. Leave for 3–4 hours.

The cheese can be stored overnight in the refrigerator but I do not advise keeping it for longer than 24 hours.

I have tried flavouring the paneer with various herbs and other flavourings: by far the best are dill and cumin.

• DILL-FLAVOURED PANEER •

• INGREDIENTS •

5–6 spears fresh dill (enough for 1 tablespoon when chopped)

225 g/7 oz unseasoned paneer, made up to the end of Step 1 above

½ teaspoon salt

Pinch of hot chilli powder

• METHOD •

Wash the dill and blot dry; pull the leaves (which are very thin, like threads) from the stems and chop very finely. When the cheese has drained for 20-30 minutes, mash in the dill with the salt and chilli powder. Either compress, as above, and eat as it is or (if made with yoghurt) knead and mould it into balls for Kumud's Deep-fried Paneer Balls (see page 62).

• CUMIN-FLAVOURED PANEER •

• INGREDIENTS •

1 scant teaspoon cumin seeds

1 large or 2 small cloves garlic

1 green chilli

225 g/7 oz unseasoned paneer,
made up to the end of Step 1 (page 59)

½ teaspoon sea salt

½ teaspoon ground turmeric

• METHOD •

Crush the cumin to a fine powder in a mortar. Peel, roughly chop, and thoroughly crush the garlic. Wash and dry the chilli, trim the stalk and slit. Remove the white inner pith and seeds and dice the flesh as finely as possible. Do not touch your eyes while handling it and wash your hands directly afterwards. When the cheese has drained, mash the prepared ingredients into it with the salt and turmeric. Press or knead and mould as before.

• KUMUD'S DEEP-FRIED •
PANEER BALLS

You can serve these as a first course or snack with crudités (such as sticks of cucumber, green pepper or celery) or as a meal accompanied by Spiced Rice (see page 39).

The paneer can be plain or flavoured, but it is essential to make it with yoghurt: with only lemon juice, the cheese disintegrates when fried.

For deep-frying you should use a saucepan small enough to economize on oil but sufficiently big to cover the source of heat: oil is highly inflammable and likely to catch fire if it spits or spills over the ring. Take care to place the pan with the handle at the back to minimize the risk of knocking it accidentally. Also check that it is completely dry before pouring in the oil, since any drops of water will cause dangerous spluttering.

Makes 14–15 balls

• INGREDIENTS •

225 g/7 oz plain or flavoured paneer made with yoghurt (see page 59), unpressed

Spiced Rice (see page 39) and/or 1 small green pepper, about ⅓ cucumber and/or 2–3 sticks of celery

600–750 ml/1–1¼ pints corn oil

4–5 small cubes of stale bread (for testing the temperature of the oil)

Smallish, thick-based saucepan large enough to cover your ring
Perforated spoon (if available)
New disposable cleaning-cloth (if available)

• METHOD •

1 After mashing the seasoning or flavourings into the paneer, divide it into 3 or 4 lumps and knead it in the palm of your

hand like dough for 10 minutes or until it is close-textured and smooth; then mould it into balls about 2.5cm/1 inch in diameter.

2 Prepare the crudités or Spiced Rice: do not start frying the balls until the rice has simmered. Wash and dry the vegetables for crudités. Quarter the pepper, remove the core, seeds and white inner pith and slice the flesh into strips. Cut the cucumber into approximately 4-cm/1½-inch lengths and cross-chop. Trim the root end and leaves from the celery, pare off any discoloured streaks and chop into convenient lengths.

3 Set a plate lined with kitchen paper to hand near the cooker. Pour oil into the smallish saucepan to a depth of at least 5 cm/2 inches and set over medium heat for 3 minutes. Gently lower a cube of bread into it using a perforated spoon, if available; otherwise use a tablespoon (to avoid splashing, do not drop it in). If the bread sizzles slightly and turns pale gold in the time it takes you to count to 60 – that is, in 1 minute – the oil has reached the right temperature for frying the balls (175°C/350°F). To maintain the temperature, reduce the heat to low (but not very low). Lower 3 or 4 balls into the pan: you should fry only a few at a time, partly so that the temperature of the oil remains constant, but also because if the balls touch each other, they will stick together. Allow to fry for 2–3 minutes or until golden: do not disturb them as they cook until the golden crust has formed, or they may break. Remove from the oil with the perforated spoon (or use a tablespoon or fish-slice) and place on the paper-lined plate. Repeat with the rest of the balls. If they brown in less than 2 minutes, lower the heat; if they take much longer, raise it. Serve hot or cold.

The oil can be reused at least once. Allow to cool and pour through a fine sieve, ideally lined with a new disposable cleaning-cloth. Without a cloth, pour gently so that the impurities stay at the bottom and throw away the last spoonful or so. Store somewhere cool in a stoppered jar or bottle.

· SHOBHNA'S PANEER ·
AND TOMATO SAUCE

Anyone who likes butter or cream, as I do, will be completely conquered by this sauce. It is not potently flavoured, although garlic and cardamom make their impact: the chief impression it gives is simply of richness. With turmeric and the orange of the tomatoes tempered by cream, plus the paneer, it looks remarkably like scrambled egg.

If the paneer is not already made, allow 3–4 hours for draining and weighting (see page 60).

Serve with plain or Shobhna's Spinach Rice (page 40).

For 3

· INGREDIENTS ·

310–375 g/10–12 oz white Basmati, Patna or American long-grain rice

Salt

400 g/13 oz ripe tomatoes

225–250 g/7–8 oz plain paneer (see page 59)

225–250 g/7–8 oz (2 fairly small or 1 largish) onion

3 cloves garlic

4 cardamom pods

Small bunch fresh coriander (enough for 1 tablespoon when chopped)

1 green chilli

2 tablespoons ghee or 1 tablespoon ghee plus 1 tablespoon oil

½ teaspoon sugar

2 teaspoons tomato purée

2 teaspoons ground turmeric

142 ml/¼ pint double cream

Saucepan with a lid (for the rice)
Wok or frying-pan

· METHOD ·

1 Rinse the rice under the cold tap until the water runs clear, put it into the saucepan with a lid and add 600 ml/1 pint salted

or unsalted water for 310 g/10 oz rice or 740 ml/1¼ pints for 375 g/12 oz. Bring to the boil, stir, cover and simmer for 18 minutes for Basmati, or 20 minutes for other types of white rice. Leave to rest, covered, for 10–15 minutes or until the sauce is ready.

2 Skin the tomatoes (see page 31) and chop fairly finely. Cut the paneer into pieces about 1.5 cm/⅔ inch square. Peel and finely chop the onion(s). Peel and roughly chop the garlic; crush to a paste in a mortar. Add the cardamoms and bruise so that the pods are open but the seeds intact. Trim the ends of the coriander stems and wash the coriander; shake off surplus water and chop finely. Wash the chilli; trim the stalk end, slit, remove the inner membrane and all or some of the seeds depending on how hot you want the sauce to be, and dice the flesh as finely as possible. Do not rub your eyes while handling it and wash your hands afterwards.

3 Warm the oil and/or ghee in the wok or frying-pan over medium heat. Add the onion and fry for 3–4 minutes or until soft but not brown, turning often. Add the chilli, garlic and cardamoms, and stir. Add the tomatoes and sugar and cook for 3–4 minutes, turning constantly and pressing the tomato flesh against the bottom of the pan until dissolved. Add the tomato purée, turmeric and 1 teaspoon salt. Lower the heat and simmer for about 5 minutes. Stir in the cream, then the paneer; sprinkle with the chopped coriander and serve.

• PANEER PULLAO •
WITH PEAS

Rather like natural cottage cheese, plain, uncooked paneer has a mild, only faintly cheese-like flavour. When fried in ghee, however, it acquires a surprisingly distinctive, rich taste. Here, this richness is emphasized by yoghurt: in Shobhna's Paneer and Tomato Sauce (see previous recipe), an even more pronounced effect is achieved with cream.

Use Basmati rice if possible. Apart from this, a few French beans and a little ghee, the pullao could hardly be cheaper.

Serve with Raita with Cucumber (page 28; optional).

For 3–4

• INGREDIENTS •

375 g/12 oz *unpodded fresh or 190 g/6 oz frozen peas*

125 g/4 oz (1 largish) *carrot*

50 g/2 oz *Kenya or other fine, stringless, green beans*

375 g/12 oz (3 smallish) *onions*

5 cloves *garlic*

4-cm/1½-inch *piece fresh root ginger*

2 green *chillies*

5 cardamom *pods*

6 black *peppercorns*

150 g/5 oz *mild, whole-milk yoghurt*

310 g/10 oz *white Basmati, Patna or American long-grain rice*

2 tablespoons *oil*

1 scant teaspoon *fennel seeds*

1 teaspoon *black mustard seeds*

5 cloves

5-cm/2-inch *stick cinnamon*

Salt

½ teaspoon *ground turmeric*

2 tablespoons *ghee*

225 g/7 oz *plain, unpressed paneer (see page 59)*

1½ teaspoons *garam masala (see page 21)*

Egg-whisk (if available)
Large saucepan with a lid
Wok or frying-pan (preferably non-stick)
Wok-scoop or spatula

• METHOD •

1 Pod fresh peas. Peel and finely dice the carrot. Top and tail and wash the beans; cut into 1-cm/½-inch lengths. Peel and finely slice the onions. Peel and thinly slice the garlic and

ginger, removing any fibrous patches on the ginger. Wash the chillies and trim the stalk ends; slit, remove the inner membrane and some of the seeds if you wish, and dice the flesh as finely as possible. Do not rub your eyes while chopping them and wash your hands afterwards.

2 Crush the peppercorns to a powder in a mortar. Add the garlic, ginger and chillies and pound to a paste. Add the cardamoms and bruise so that the pods are open. Whisk the yoghurt until completely homogenous; if you have no egg-whisk, beat thoroughly with a fork.

3 Rinse the rice in a sieve under the cold tap until the water runs clear; leave to drain. Warm the oil in the large saucepan over medium heat and fry the onions for 5–6 minutes or until soft and just beginning to change colour; turn often, especially towards the end. Lower the heat: if you have an electric ring which takes time to cool, remove the pan from the heat for a moment or two (or change rings). Add the fennel and mustard seeds, cloves, cinnamon, one generous teaspoon salt and the turmeric and stir; add the flavourings in the mortar and stir for a few seconds. Add the rice and stir until thoroughly mixed. Turn the yoghurt into the pan and stir until it is absorbed. Add 600 ml/1 pint water, the beans and the carrots and bring to the boil. Lower the heat, stir, cover and simmer gently for 18 minutes for Basmati rice or 20 minutes for other types of white rice; remove from the heat and leave to rest, covered, for 10 minutes.

4 While the rice simmers, cook the peas: just cover with slightly salted boiling water and boil for 2 minutes if frozen or 5–10 minutes if fresh (the time they take to cook varies widely according to age and size). Drain and return to the hot saucepan.

5 When the rice has rested for 5 minutes or more, warm the ghee in the wok or frying-pan over fairly low heat. Add the paneer and stir until it has melted to the consistency of scrambled eggs. Reduce the heat to the lowest possible, cover and leave for 3–4 minutes. Stir the ghee-flavoured paneer into the rice with as much of any brown crust at the bottom of the saucepan as you can scrape off with the scoop. Stir the peas into the pullao, sprinkle with the garam masala and serve immediately.

· DEEP-FRIED TOFU ·
BALLS WITH GINGER

I first had something like these at the Cantonese restaurant, Poons, in London's Covent Garden. Nobody else with whom I was dining liked them because of the blandness of the beancurd (they were meant to be eaten with pungent dishes such as hot-and-sour prawns); however, I loved them for their smooth, almost creamy centres and crisp skin. This version is by no means the same, partly because I have flavoured it with sherry and ginger; I have also settled for a variegated texture, since I find that this works best with the tofu that you are likely to be able to buy in ordinary supermarkets.

To give an extra dimension to the flavour, non-vegetarians may like to replace half the tofu with prawns (see page 70).

As with Kumud's Deep-fried Paneer Balls, deep-fried tofu can be served alone as a snack or as first course, in which case accompany them with Red-Chilli Oil (see page 35); alternatively they can form part of a main course with Fried Rice with Beans and Red Pepper (page 42) or plain rice plus another dish, such as Stir-Fried Mushrooms and Green Pepper with Celery (page 96): as the tofu is rich in protein, a vegetable-only dish is perfectly adequate.

The exact amount of cornflour needed varies according to the size of the egg and how completely you separate it: if you leave a little white with the yolk, the mixture will be relatively stiff and less flour will be absorbed. The yolk is not required for this recipe: if possible, use it for scrambled eggs. Store it, covered, in the refrigerator, but do not keep it for longer than 24 hours.

The pan in which you fry the balls should be fairly small to save oil but large enough to cover your ring completely, as hot oil is inflammable. Check that it is perfectly dry before you pour in the oil, otherwise it might splutter, and place it with the handle towards the back of the stove to reduce the risk of accidents.

Makes 12–14 balls

• INGREDIENTS •

250 g/8 oz plain tofu

1 large or 2 small cloves garlic

2.5-cm/1-inch piece fresh root ginger

1 size 2 egg (white only)

Salt

½ teaspoon hot chilli powder

2 teaspoons medium-dry sherry

40–60 g/1½– 2 oz cornflour

520–600 ml/17 fl oz–1 pint corn oil

4–5 small cubes of stale bread (for testing the temperature of the oil)

Egg-whisk (if available)
Smallish, thick-based saucepan large enough to cover your ring
Perforated spoon (if available)

• METHOD •

1 Wash the tofu in cold water. If there is a piece of the block left over, either follow the instructions on the packet for keeping it or put it into a bowl, submerge in cold water, cover and store for up to 3 days in the refrigerator. Squeeze the portion to be used in kitchen paper to extract as much moisture as possible and cut in half. Mash one half with a fork until it resembles moderately fine breadcrumbs; cut the other half into 4–5 mm/less than ¼ inch dice.

2 Peel and roughly chop the garlic and ginger, removing any fibrous patches on the ginger (if necessary, make up the quantity with more). Crush to a smooth paste in a mortar. Separate the egg: crack it sharply in the middle, hold over a smallish bowl and tip the yolk from one half of the shell to the other until all (or most) of the white has fallen out. To keep the yolk until next day, put it into a cup, cover and store in the refrigerator. Add a very little salt to the white and whisk until stiff and opaque: if you have no egg-whisk, use it as it is (whisking lightens the balls and improves their texture, but it is not essential). Add the crushed garlic and ginger, chilli powder, sherry, 1½ teaspoons salt and 40g/1½ oz cornflour; mix thoroughly. Stir in the mashed and chopped tofu. The mixture should be stiff enough to mould into neat balls: if it is sticky, add more cornflour. Mould into balls about 2.5–3 cm/1–1¼ inches across (about the size of lychees).

3 Pour oil into the saucepan to a depth of at least 5 cm/ 2 inches and place over medium/high heat for 3 minutes. Meanwhile, set a plate lined with kitchen paper to hand near the cooker. Gently lower one of the cubes of bread into the pan with the perforated spoon if available (otherwise use a tablespoon); take care not to cause splashing. When the oil is hot enough to fry the balls, the bread will have turned gold by the time you have counted 20 – that is, in 20 seconds (it should be 190°C/375°F). Reduce the heat to fairly low to maintain the temperature and gently immerse one of the balls: add up to 3 more at intervals of a few seconds. Fry for 1–1½ minutes each or until golden-brown: do not turn more than is necessary to keep the balls separate (they have a tendency to cluster together). Remove each ball as it is ready and set on the plate lined with kitchen paper. Continue in this way until all the balls are fried. If you wish, you can give them an extra-crisp crust by refrying them for just 1 or 2 seconds. Serve promptly.

• DEEP-FRIED TOFU •
AND PRAWN BALLS

These are made in exactly the same way as above but with 250 g/8 oz unshelled or 125 g/4 oz shelled prawns instead of 125 g/4 oz chopped tofu.

They will taste more of prawn if you use fresh – that is, chilled rather than frozen ones. For maximum flavour, use prawns still in their shells. If you do use frozen ones, remember to allow several hours for defrosting.

• METHOD •

Shell the prawns if necessary. Pull off the head of each one and the shell from the tail; pick off the remaining shell from the body. Rinse chilled prawns in cold water and leave to dry in a sieve or blot with paper; drain and dry frozen ones. Chop into slices 5 mm/less than ¼ inch thick. Mix with 125 g/4 oz mashed tofu; add the egg white, flavourings and cornflour, mould into balls and deep-fry as before (see above).

· FRIED RICE WITH ·
AUBERGINE AND TOFU

For a light, dry result the rice must be simmered for 45 minutes or more ahead of time to give the moisture time to evaporate: if fried while still damp, it will be heavy and soggy. It is desirable rather than otherwise to leave it until cold because this means that it will be really dry: if you like, cook it the previous day.

The aubergine should be firm: if spongy it is old and may become mushy when fried. To reduce the amount of oil needed to fry it, leave it to sweat (see page 16) for at least 30 minutes prior to cooking.

Serve with Red-Chilli Oil (optional).

For 3

· INGREDIENTS ·

310 g/10 oz Thai fragrant or white Patna or American long-grain rice

Salt, some of which should be finely ground

250–310 g/8–10 oz (1 medium) aubergine

250 g/8 oz unpodded or 125 g/4 oz frozen peas

190–200 g/6–6½ oz tofu

Small bunch coriander (enough for 2 tablespoons when chopped)

125 g/4 oz button mushrooms

150 g/5 oz (1 medium) onion

2 cloves garlic

2-cm/¾-inch piece fresh root ginger

1 mild or moderately hot green chilli

4 tablespoons oil

2 tablespoons light soy sauce

Saucepan with a lid (for the rice)
Large wok or frying-pan
Fish-slice or perforated spoon
Wok-scoop or spatula

• METHOD •

1 Rinse the rice under the cold tap until the water runs clear, put into the saucepan with a lid and add 600ml/1 pint water, with or without salt. Bring to the boil, stir, cover and simmer for 12 minutes for Thai or 20 minutes for other types of rice. Leave to rest, covered, for at least 45 minutes. (If you are cooking it a day in advance, allow to become cold, cover and store in the refrigerator.)

2 Wash the aubergine, trim the ends and cut into 2-cm/¾-inch slices; then cross-chop into sticks 5–6 mm/¼ inch wide. Sprinkle with fine salt and leave for 30 minutes–1 hour in a sieve or colander to sweat. Rinse under the cold tap; leave on a plate lined with kitchen paper to dry.

3 Shell the peas if necessary. Cover with salted water and boil for 2 minutes if frozen or 5–15 minutes if fresh (the time they take varies according age and size). Drain and set aside.

4 Unless you have a 190- or 200-g/6- or 6½-oz block, cut off the tofu you will need and store the rest: follow the instructions on the packet or immerse in cold water, cover and keep in the refrigerator for up to 3 days. Wash the piece to be used in cold water, squeeze in kitchen paper to remove surplus moisture and cut into sticks the same size as the aubergine. Set on another plate lined with kitchen paper. Trim the ends of the coriander stems; wash, shake or blot dry and chop. Trim the mushroom stalks and wash and dry the mushrooms; slice finely. Peel and finely chop the onion. Peel and thinly slice the garlic and ginger, discarding any fibrous patches on the ginger. Wash and dry the chilli, trim the stalk end and slit; remove the white inner membrane and seeds and dice the flesh as finely as possible. Do not rub your eyes while handling it and wash your hands directly afterwards.

5 Set an empty plate to hand near the cooker. Warm 2 tablespoons of the oil in the wok or frying-pán over medium heat, add the tofu and fry for 3–4 minutes or until pale gold. Remove the pan from the heat and transfer the tofu to the plate with the fish-slice or perforated spoon; leave the oil in the pan.

6 Loosen the rice with a fork. Put all the prepared ingredients plus the soy sauce to hand near the cooker. Add the remaining 2 tablespoons oil to the wok and warm over high heat. Add the

ginger and garlic and allow to fry until just beginning to change colour. Add the aubergine and stir-fry for 2 minutes. Add the onion and stir for 30 seconds. Add the mushrooms and stir for 1½–2 minutes; add the chilli and stir briefly. Reduce the heat to medium: if your ring cools slowly, change to another. Turn the rice into the pan and stir for another 1½–2 minutes, using the wok-scoop or spatula. Add the tofu and stir; add the peas and stir. Stir in the soy sauce and cook for a few seconds; add and stir in the coriander. Serve immediately.

• EGG DISHES •

Eggs are used in Indian and Far-Eastern cooking in many ways which are similar to European – for example, omelettes and versions of scrambled eggs (see Shehzad's Eggs with Chilli and Coriander, which is similar to a European piperade). However, as they are cheaper than meat, Far-Eastern cooks often combine them with it to make the meat go further (as in Thai-style Pork with Eggs or, in a rather different way, Yan-Kit So's Steak Omelette, where beef replaces the ham or prawns we would expect). Among other ways of cooking eggs, which for reasons of space I have not included here, are fried in rice or stirred into strings in soup. All these uses have the advantage over many of the traditional European methods that the eggs are cooked until set, which means that they are heated sufficiently to kill bacteria.

Throughout the book, I have used free-range eggs: anyone who has seen the conditions in which battery hens are kept will understand why. Free-range hens, in contrast, have access to grass and the open air and are guaranteed a fairly generous minimum of space (ten square metres per head). Quite apart from this, their eggs are well worth the extra cost in terms of taste. To make the most of the flavour, however, as well as for health reasons, you should ensure that they are really fresh, which is now very easy since every egg is date-stamped.

· SHEHZAD'S EGGS WITH · CHILLI AND CORIANDER

There are any number of recipes in Indian cookery for curry-type egg dishes of one sort or another. The only hot ingredient in this one is chillies: these, plus the coriander, give sufficient strength of flavour for the eggs to be eaten like curry with rice but do not make it too potent to serve with toast or hot, crusty bread for a less substantial meal.

This recipe takes less than 10 minutes to cook and 10–15 to prepare – that is, altogether about the time (white) rice takes to cook. If you want to serve it with hot toast, someone else should make the toast while you cook the eggs.

For 3 as a main meal or 4 (with bread or toast) for brunch

· INGREDIENTS ·

375 g/12 oz white Basmati, Patna or American long-grain rice, or bread or toast

Salt

2 medium-sized ripe tomatoes

190 g/6 oz (1 medium/largish) onion

3 cloves garlic

2–3 sprigs fresh coriander (enough for 1 dessertspoon when chopped)

1 green chilli

1 small fresh or dried red chilli

4 eggs

1 tablespoon oil

2 tablespoons ghee

Saucepan with a lid (for the rice)
Wok or frying-pan
Wok-scoop or wooden spoon

· METHOD ·

1 If you are serving the eggs with rice, rinse the rice in a sieve under the cold tap until the water runs clear. Put it into the saucepan with a lid, add 675 ml/1⅛ pints cold water and, if you wish, ⅓ teaspoon salt. Bring to the boil and stir. Reduce the

heat to a simmer, cover and simmer for 18 minutes for Basmati or 20 minutes for other types of rice. Leave to rest, covered, for 5–10 minutes.

2 Skin the tomatoes (see page 31) and chop, discarding the cores. Peel and finely slice the onions. Peel and crush the garlic. Wash the coriander, blot dry with kitchen paper and roughly chop. Wash and dry the chillies; trim off the stalk ends, slit, remove the seeds and inner membranes and dice the flesh as finely as possible. Do not touch your eyes while handling them and wash your hands directly afterwards. Break the eggs into a bowl and beat with a fork until homogenous; wash your hands again.

3 Warm the oil and ghee in the wok or frying-pan over medium heat. Add the onion and fry for 7–8 minutes or until an even golden brown; turn constantly, particularly towards the end (a wok is helpful in frying it evenly because any pieces which become too coloured can be pushed up the side). Lower the heat slightly: if you have electric rings which respond slowly to a change of setting, cool the pan by removing it from the heat for a moment or two. Add the red chilli, crushed garlic and 1 teaspoon salt and stir. Add the tomatoes and cook for 3–5 minutes, pressing the flesh against the bottom of the pan until dissolved.

If you are planning to serve toast, it should be made now.

4 Add about a quarter of the green chilli, coriander and beaten eggs. Using the wok-scoop or wooden spoon, stir-fry, turning from the bottom upwards, until the egg begins to set; add another quarter and repeat until all the egg is just set: if it remains liquid, it is not cooked enough to kill bacteria. Serve immediately.

• CHINESE OMELETTE •

Chinese omelettes are different from Western ones in that the filling is mixed with the raw egg rather than added when the egg is in the pan. Also, instead of being left with a slightly soft, creamy middle, the egg is cooked until fully set, which from the health point of view is a much better option.

As in the West, any number of fillings (or rather, additions) are possible: on the following pages are two which are a little more unexpected than the usual cheese, ham, prawns or mushrooms.

• YAN-KIT'S STEAK OMELETTE •

When I discussed this book with the cookery writer Yan-kit So, she at once suggested this recipe from her recent *Classic Food of China* (Macmillan), not because it is quick and easy or an economical way of serving steak, but for its nutritional value, since she is convinced that students and other young people do not eat enough protein (she is very decidedly opposed to vegetarianism).

Sesame oil is a pleasant finishing touch if you have any, but not essential.

Serve with crudités, such as cucumber, celery and green pepper (see page 133).

For 2

• INGREDIENTS •

200 g/6½ oz Thai fragrant or brown Patna or American long-grain rice

Salt

190 g/6 oz rump steak (for preference) or minute steak, thinly cut

Pepper

1 teaspoon soy sauce

1 teaspoon medium-dry sherry

Pinch of sugar

½ teaspoon cornflour

4 tablespoons oil

3 eggs

2 spring onions

1 teaspoon sesame oil (optional)

Saucepan with a lid (for the rice)
Sharp knife for cutting the steak
Large wok or frying-pan (preferably non-stick)
Fish-slice or perforated spoon
Wok-scoop or spatula

• METHOD •

1 Set the rice to cook. Rinse under the cold tap until the water runs clear, put into the saucepan with a lid and add 360 ml/ ⅗ pint salted or unsalted water. Bring to the boil, stir, cover and simmer for 12 minutes for Thai or 30 minutes for brown rice. Leave to rest, covered, for 10 minutes.

2 Wash the steak in cold water, trim off all visible fat and cut the lean meat into strips 2.5 cm/1 inch long and 6 mm/¼ inch wide. Lay on a plate and season moderately with pepper. Beat together the soy sauce, sherry, sugar, cornflour and ¼ teaspoon salt. Pour over the meat and toss to mix. Add 3 teaspoons water and continue to toss until all the liquid is absorbed. Leave to rest while the rice cooks or for 15–20 minutes.

3 Place an empty plate to hand near the cooker. Warm the oil in the wok or frying-pan over high heat for about 1 minute. Add the beef and stir-fry until just seared – that is, brownish rather than red but not browned: there should still be a little pink liquid oozing from it. Yan-kit is careful to say that if you like your beef well cooked, you should fry it for a little longer; however, this will mean that the omelette will have less flavour. Remove the pan from the heat and quickly transfer the meat with the fish-slice or perforated spoon to the plate; leave the oil in the pan. Allow the beef to cool for a minute or two while you prepare the eggs.

4 Break the eggs into a cup or bowl, add a fairly generous seasoning of salt and pepper and beat with a fork until homogenous. Trim the roots and green leaves from the onions; peel off and discard the outer layer and slice finely. Add to the eggs (ideally, you should use the green parts only, but I leave that to you). Stir in the beef.

5 Reheat the oil over a medium flame for a few seconds; if using a wok, tip it so that the oil coats the sides. Pour in the beef-and-egg mixture. Tilt the pan so that the liquid egg spreads over the bottom; stir it back towards the middle with the wok-scoop or spatula. Repeat, spreading the egg over a wide area of the wok, or over the whole base if using a frying-pan, until it has set at the bottom. Continue to cook until the top is firm. Sprinkle with the sesame oil, if you have any, and serve immediately with the rice (as the omelette is for 2 people, you will have to cut it in half).

• TOFU OMELETTE •

You can serve this either with plain rice and crudités, as for Steak Omelette, or accompanied by Fried Rice with Beans and Red Pepper, in which case, as the fried rice is strongly flavoured with soy sauce, I suggest omitting soy from the omelette. Prepare the eggs and tofu before frying the rice and make the omelette immediately afterwards.

For 2

• INGREDIENTS •

200 g/6½ oz Thai fragrant rice or
Fried Rice with Beans and Red
Pepper made with 200 g/6½ oz rice,
40 g/1½ oz beans, ½ red pepper,
50 g/2 oz mushrooms, 1 stick celery,
1 tablespoon plus 2 teaspoons soy
sauce and the other ingredients
given (see page 42)

Salt

100 g/3½ oz plain tofu

Pepper

2 teaspoons soy sauce (if serving with
plain rice)

2 cloves garlic

2 tablespoons oil

3 eggs

Few sprigs coriander (enough for 1
dessertspoon when chopped)

Saucepan with a lid (for the rice)
Large wok or frying-pan (preferably non-stick)
Fish-slice or perforated spoon
Wok-scoop or spatula

• METHOD •

1 Set the rice to cook. For fried rice, see page 42. For plain rice, wash the rice under the cold tap until the water runs clear, put into the saucepan with a lid and add 360 ml/⅗ pint salted or unsalted water. Bring to the boil, stir, cover and simmer for 12 minutes. Leave to rest, covered, for 10 minutes.

2 Cut as much tofu as you need from the block and store the rest: follow the instructions on the packet or immerse in cold water, cover and keep for up to 3 days in the refrigerator. Wash

the piece to be used in cold water and squeeze in kitchen paper to remove surplus moisture. Cut into sticks 2 cm/¾ inch long and 5 mm/less than ¼ inch wide. Season lightly with salt and pepper. If you are serving the omelette with plain rice, sprinkle the tofu with the soy sauce, toss to mix, and leave for 10–15 minutes.

3 Peel and finely slice the garlic. Set an empty place to hand by the cooker. Warm the oil in the wok or frying-pan over high heat; add the garlic and allow to fry for 30 seconds or until beginning to colour. Add the tofu and stir-fry for 2 minutes or until pale gold. Remove the pan from the heat and transfer both the tofu and garlic to the plate with the fish-slice or perforated spoon, leaving the oil in the pan.

4 Break the eggs into a cup or bowl, sprinkle generously with salt and pepper and beat with a fork until homogenous. Stir in the tofu. Trim the ends of the coriander stems; wash the coriander, blot dry and chop finely.

5 If you are serving fried rice, fry it now; keep it warm while you make the omelette by leaving it in the pan in which it was cooked. Check that there are no fragments of tofu or garlic in the wok or frying-pan. Reheat the oil over a medium flame for a few seconds; if using a wok, tip it so that the oil coats the sides. Pour in the egg-and-tofu mixture. Tilt the pan to spread the egg as before. Stir it back towards the middle with the wok-scoop or spatula; repeat until all the egg at the bottom is set. Cook until the egg on the top of the omelette is just firm, sprinkle with the coriander, fold and serve.

• STEAMED EGGS •

In the Far East, this would be made with stock; however, milk is more convenient and nutritious, and gives a thicker, more popular texture. If you like, you can add a little cream. With milk, the dish is simply savoury custard, but unlike boiled custard, the eggs are cooked until set, which means that they are heated sufficiently to kill bacteria.

When made with stock, various additions are often stirred into the eggs before cooking (see books by Madhur Jaffrey and

Kenneth Lo: page 193). For the milk version, however, I recommend either prawns or just a scattering of spring onion over the top. Serve accompanied by Fried Rice with Beans and Red Pepper (page 42).

To make an elegant dish, you need a small, shallow ovenproof dish (for a pudding for 2, about 15 cm/6 inches across and 4 cm/1½ inches deep) and either a steamer or a wok with a lid plus something on which to set the dish. Less demanding in terms of equipment is to use an ordinary pudding basin fitted into a saucepan, as in the directions given below.

Fresh (that is, chilled) prawns have more flavour than frozen; best of all, use prawns still in their shells. Allow several hours for frozen ones to defrost.

For 2

• INGREDIENTS •

190–225 g/6–7 oz Thai fragrant or white Patna or American long-grain rice or Fried Rice with Beans and Red Pepper (page 42), made with 200 g/6½ oz rice, 40 g/1½ oz beans, ½ red pepper, 50 g/2 oz mushrooms, 1 stick celery, 1 tablespoon plus 2 teaspoons soy sauce and the other ingredients as given

Salt

50 g/2 oz prawns (optional)

2 eggs

Pepper

Chilli powder

1 tablespoon light soy sauce

225 ml/7½ fl oz milk

1 spring onion (optional)

Saucepan with a lid (for the rice)
Pudding basin 16 cm/6¼ inches across the top
from the outside rim
Saucepan 16 cm/6¼ inch (deep), with a lid if possible

• METHOD •

1 For plain rice, rinse the rice until the water runs clear and put into the saucepan with a lid. Add 340 ml/just over ½ pint water for 190 g/6 oz rice or 400 ml/⅔ pint for 225 g/7 oz, plus a little salt if you wish. Bring to the boil, stir, cover and simmer for 12 minutes for Thai or 20 minutes for other types of rice.

Leave to stand, covered, while the eggs steam. If you are serving fried rice, start frying when the eggs are ready.

2 If you are using fresh prawns, shell them if necessary: pull off the heads and the shell from the tails; pick off the remaining shell over the body. Wash and set on kitchen paper to dry. If using shelled prawns, wash and dry them. If the prawns are frozen, drain and dry them. Chop into 1-cm/½-inch lengths.

3 Beat the eggs with a fork until completely homogenous but not frothy. Season generously with salt and pepper. Add a sprinkling of chilli powder and the soy sauce; stir in the milk.

4 Fill the 16-cm/6¼-inch saucepan one-third full of water; set the basin in it to ensure that it does not overflow, remove and put the water on to boil. When the water boils, reduce the heat to a simmer; beat the egg mixture again, stir in the prawns if you are using them, and pour into the basin. Put the basin into the saucepan and cover the top of both basin and pan with cooking-foil so that steam cannot escape. Put the lid on the saucepan and steam for 15 minutes. When ready, the egg should be set all through. To test it, insert a knife or skewer into the middle: it should come out clean. Steam for a little longer if necessary.

5 While the eggs cook, cut off the roots and the upper leaves of the spring onion (the lower part of the leaves will add colour to the pudding); peel off the outer layers and slippery underskin, chop into 1-cm/½-inch slices and cut lengthways into sticks. Sprinkle over the top of the pudding when cooked.

• THAI-STYLE PORK •
WITH EGGS

I owe this recipe, or at least the gist of it, to the cookery writer and restaurateur Vatcharin Bhumichitr: I first made it after enjoying a similar dish at his restaurant, Chaing Mai, in Soho (London). The following differs from his version not least in that I have substituted beans and celery for bamboo shoots and straw mushrooms, and added an extra egg.

The eggs are stir-fried and hence shredded, and impregnated with sauce so that you might almost mistake them for some kind of rich-tasting fish or white meat.

Partly because the vegetables are quick to chop, the dish can be entirely prepared while the rice (Thai) cooks and rests – that is, in 20–25 minutes.

As you will not need the fat, choose lean pork: chops should be loin rather than shoulder or chump.

Serve with crudités, such as strips of cucumber and green pepper (see page 133) and Red-Chilli Oil (page 35).

For 2–3

• INGREDIENTS •

200–310 g/6½–10 oz Thai fragrant, white Patna or American long-grain rice

Salt

250 g/8 oz pork chops, preferably thinly cut

2 large or 3 smaller sticks celery

75 g/2½ oz Kenya or other fine, stringless, green beans

3 spring onions

2 cloves garlic

½ lemon

2 eggs

Pepper

3 tablespoons oil

1 tablespoon fish sauce

2 tablespoons soy sauce

Saucepan with a lid (for the rice)
Sharp knife (for chopping the pork)
Wok or frying-pan
Wok-scoop or spatula

• METHOD •

1 Rinse the rice, put into the saucepan with a lid, add 400 ml/ ⅔ pint salted or unsalted water for 200 g/6½ oz rice or 600 ml/ 1 pint for 310 g/10 oz. Bring to the boil, stir, cover and simmer for 12 minutes for Thai or 20 minutes for other types of rice. Leave to rest, covered, for 10 minutes.

2 Cut the bones (if any) and all the visible fat from the pork. Wash in cold water, dry and chop into strips 2 cm/¾ inch long

and 5 mm/less than ¼ inch wide. Trim the leaves and root ends from the celery and pare off any brownish streaks; wash, dry, cut into 2-cm/¾-inch slices and cross-chop into sticks of the same width as the pork. Top and tail and wash the beans; chop into 2-cm/¾-inch lengths. Trim the leaves and roots from the onions, peel off the outer layer, slice into 1-cm/½-inch lengths and cross-chop into shreds. Peel and finely slice the garlic; squeeze the lemon. Break the eggs into a cup or bowl, season lightly with salt and fairly generously with pepper and beat with a fork until homogenous.

3 Warm the oil in the wok or frying-pan over high heat, add the garlic and allow to fry until just starting to colour. Add the pork and stir-fry for 30 seconds or until pale and opaque. Add the eggs and stir until just set; add the beans and celery and stir for 1 minute. Add the fish sauce, soy sauce and 1 tablespoon water and stir for 2 minutes. Add and stir in 3 teaspoons lemon juice; taste the sauce (cautiously, since it will be very hot) and add another teaspoon of lemon juice if you wish. Sprinkle with the spring onions and serve with the rice.

· VEGETABLE AND ·
PULSE DISHES

Certainly in the past, although happily the situation in this country is now improving, vegetables were much more highly regarded in Asia than in Britain. Today they continue to play a major role in Asian cooking, not only because of their cheapness in relation to meat and the number of vegetarians in the East, but also because of the pattern of meal imposed, or at least encouraged, by rice. In Far-Eastern cooking in particular, no one dish is regarded as superior to another nor, in general, are meat and vegetables cooked separately. Typically, a little meat (often pork) is added to vegetables to give them added flavour or (in the same way as eggs) vegetables are added to meat to make it go further. This is less true of Indian cookery, but even in India vegetables are cooked with great care and attention.

Pulses are also of great importance in India, where a vegetarian dinner would not be considered complete without a dish of beans or lentils. Eating them with rice might sound like an undesirably solid combination, but, in terms of taste, it is surprisingly successful because pulses, like potatoes (which Indians also favour), react extremely well to spicing.

For the benefit of vegetarians, I have not placed any dishes containing meat (or fish) in this chapter; instead, the recipes here contain pulses, nuts or tofu.

• INDIAN KEDGEREE •

The original, Indian version of kedgeree is a very simple dish made with lentils rather than fish and eggs. The following is loosely based on a recipe given by Dharamjit Singh in his classic book *Indian Cookery* (Penguin, 1970): his version is intended to be 'very light and digestible'. Apart from replacing the butter he specifies with ghee and oil, I have added a little more flavouring, recommended using two sorts of lentils to give greater textural interest, and suggested serving the kedgeree with lemon juice and Onion Chips (page 27). The rice, which is simmered for much longer than usual, ends up soft but deliciously succulent and fluffy: in this recipe, particularly, Basmati is well worth the extra cost. Apart from this, the dish could hardly be cheaper.

Allow about an hour for the rice and lentils to soak. The cooking time is 1¼–1½ hours.

For 4

• INGREDIENTS •

125 g/4 oz green lentils	2 green chillies
125 g/4 oz split red lentils	2 tablespoons ghee
250 g/8 oz white Basmati rice	2 tablespoons oil
375 g/12 oz (3 medium) onions	1 slightly rounded teaspoon salt
1 teaspoon coriander seeds	2 bayleaves
4 black peppercorns	½ lemon
4-cm/1½-inch piece fresh root ginger	Onion Chips to serve (see page 27)

Large saucepan with a lid

• METHOD •

1 Pick over the lentils, put into a bowl with the rice and cover with water (you will need at least 600 ml/1 pint). Leave for about an hour.

2 Peel and finely chop the onions. Crush the coriander and peppercorns in a mortar. Peel and roughly chop the ginger, removing any fibrous patches; add to the spices in the mortar and crush to a paste. Wash and dry the chillies. Trim the stalk ends, slit and, unless you think that they are very mild or want a relatively hot result, pick out all the seeds. Remove the inner membrane and finely dice the flesh. Do not touch your eyes while handling them and wash your hands afterwards.

3 Drain the rice and lentils and rinse under the cold tap until the water runs clear. Warm the ghee and oil in the large saucepan and fry the onions over medium heat for 6 minutes or until pale but not deep gold. Reduce the heat to low: if your ring responds to a change of setting slowly, remove the pan to cool it for a moment or two. Add the lentils and rice and stir-fry for 8–10 minutes, until the rice looks slightly contracted and smells distinctly fried. Stir in the chillies, add the crushed flavourings and stir-fry for a few seconds. Add 1.1 litres/2 pints water, the salt and the bayleaves, bring to the boil and boil briskly for 2 minutes. Lower the heat, stir thoroughly but gently, cover and simmer as gently as possible for 50 minutes–1 hour. Allow to rest, covered, for 10–15 minutes. Sprinkle with lemon juice and serve with Onion Chips.

• SHEHZAD'S RED KIDNEY • BEAN CURRY

Red kidney beans, because of their slight sweetness, make an excellent basis for curry. Shehzad's version is particularly full- and rich-flavoured, partly as a result of long, slow cooking, which gives the spices time to blend and mellow.

Unfortunately in view of the cooking-time (nearly 2 hours), the curry cannot be made the day before: if left overnight, the beans become mushy and the flavour deteriorates. Do not forget to set the beans to soak overnight.

For 4

• INGREDIENTS •

125 g/4 oz red kidney beans, soaked in cold water overnight

Salt

500 g/1 lb ripe tomatoes or 397-g/14-oz tin tomatoes

About 200 g/6½ oz (1 largish) onion

3 cloves garlic

4-cm/1½-inch piece fresh root ginger

3 tablespoons oil

1 bayleaf

5-cm/2-inch stick cinnamon

2 cloves

1 teaspoon hot chilli powder

¼ teaspoon ground turmeric

400–450 g/13–14 oz white Patna, Basmati or American long-grain rice

Wok or large saucepan with a lid
Small saucepan with a lid

• METHOD •

1 Put the beans into the small saucepan with a lid and cover with water (do not add salt). Bring to the boil, boil briskly for 10 minutes and drain. (The beans contain toxin in their skins which is removed by boiling: changing the water is an additional precaution.) Return the beans to the saucepan, just cover with fresh water (still without salt) and bring to the boil. Cover and simmer for 25 minutes; add a little salt and continue to simmer for 5–15 minutes or until tender but not soft. Drain over a bowl to catch the liquor. Make up the liquor to 300 ml/ ½ pint with water.

2 While the beans simmer, skin the tomatoes (see page 00) and chop. Peel and finely slice the onion. Peel and roughly chop the garlic and ginger, discarding any fibrous patches on the ginger; crush to a paste in a mortar.

3 Warm the oil in the wok or large saucepan over moderate/ lowish heat. Throw in the bayleaf, cinnamon and cloves (whole) and turn for a few seconds in the oil. Add the onion and fry for 7–8 minutes or until an even pale brown, turning often, especially towards the end. Lower the heat: if your ring is electric and slow to respond to a change of setting, remove the pan from the heat to cool it for a moment or two. Add the garlic and ginger, chilli powder and turmeric and fry for 20–30 seconds. Add the tomatoes, season with 1 teaspoon salt and cook for 7–10 minutes, pressing the flesh against the bottom of the pan until liquefied. Add the beans and bean liquor, bring just to the boil and reduce the heat to a simmer. Cover and simmer gently for 1 hour 10 minutes or until the sauce is rich and thick.

4 Set the rice to cook while the curry simmers. Rinse under the cold tap until the water runs clear, add 800 or 900 ml/1⅓ or 1½ pints salted or unsalted water according to whether you are using 400 g/13 oz or 450 g/14 oz rice and bring to the boil. Stir, cover and simmer for 18 minutes for white Basmati, or 20 minutes for other types of white rice. Leave to rest, covered, for 10 minutes. Serve with the curry.

• TOMATOES STUFFED WITH • MINT AND WALNUTS

This is adapted from a cookery book written by and for the Indian community in East Africa, *Anpurna Part* 4 (Shree Oshwal Mahila Mandal), which is full of ideas and recipes of a sort that I have not found published in this country.

The stuffing is rich but the richness is offset by the mint (since I have included a much higher proportion of walnuts, this version contains more protein than the original, which was presumably intended as one out of several dishes to be served at a meal: another would probably have been beans or lentils).

You will need very large 'beef' or Mediterranean (often labelled 'slicing' or 'baking') tomatoes. In giving quantities I have assumed that they will weigh at least 250 g/8 oz each.

Use stale bread for the breadcrumbs: fresh bread tends to form doughy lumps when grated.

Serve with Raita with Cucumber and Mint (page 29).
 For 4

• INGREDIENTS •

50 g/2 oz stale bread

125 g/4 oz (1 smallish) onion

1 sprig mint (enough for 1 level
tablespoon when chopped)

100 g/3½ oz walnuts or walnut
pieces

310 g/10 oz white or brown
Basmati, Patna or American long-
grain rice

Salt

4 large tomatoes weighing about
1 kg/2 lb in total

Pepper

A little sugar

20–25 g/¾–1 oz butter

Grater
Saucepan with a lid (for the rice)
Medium-sized, shallow ovenproof dish

• METHOD •

1 Finely grate the bread. Peel and coarsely grate the onion. Wash the mint, pull off the leaves, blot dry and chop finely. Crush the walnuts fairly finely.

2 Rinse the rice until the water runs clear and put into the saucepan with a lid. Add 600 ml/1 pint water, with salt if you wish, and bring to the boil. Stir, cover and simmer for 18 minutes for white Basmati, 20 minutes for other types of white rice, or 30 minutes for brown. Leave to stand, covered, for 10–15 minutes.

3 Pre-heat the oven to 200°C/400°F/Gas Mark 6; lightly butter the ovenproof dish. Wash the tomatoes and cut off the tops. Scoop out the cores and the soft, juicy flesh around the seeds. Throw away the cores; mix the flesh with the breadcrumbs, mint, onion and walnuts. Season generously with salt and pepper and beat thoroughly together with a fork. Sprinkle the hollowed-out insides of the tomatoes with a little salt and pepper and a pinch of sugar. Fill with the stuffing, put into the dish, add a knob of butter to the top of each and bake in the

oven for 20–25 minutes, until just beginning to ooze juice: do not cook them longer or they may collapse when served.

• SWEET-AND-SOUR •
AUBERGINE WITH PEANUTS AND BEANSPROUTS

In this dish a fairly potent sauce emphasizes the sweetness of the pepper and the richness of the aubergine; beans pick up the sour element, and the nuts and beansprouts add crispness (and protein).

If you have no choice, use mung beansprouts; however, mixed sprouts, which can sometimes be bought at supermarkets or health-food shops, will give a more interesting result.

Both the aubergine and the pepper should be firm and glossy: if the aubergine is soft and wrinkled, it is old and may become mushy when fried.

Aubergines are very absorbent, which means that they take up a relatively large amount of oil when fried. This can be modified by drawing out some of their moisture with salt: it is desirable to leave them to sweat for at least 30 minutes before cooking.

For 3–4

• INGREDIENTS •

375 g/12 oz (1 medium) aubergine

Salt, some of which should be finely ground

190 g/6 oz mixed (for preference) or mung beansprouts

310–400 g/10–13 oz Thai fragrant or white Patna or American long-grain rice

1 red pepper

190 g/6 oz (1 medium to largish) onion

75 g/2½ oz Kenya or other fine, stringless, green beans

2 cloves garlic

2-cm/¾-inch piece fresh root ginger

½ lemon

1 tablespoon dark soy sauce

1 tablespoon white-wine vinegar

2 teaspoons cornflour

60 g/generous 2 oz (2 slightly rounded tablespoons) soft dark-brown sugar

2 tablespoons vegetable stock or water

5 tablespoons oil

2 tablespoons medium-dry sherry

50 g/2 oz unsalted peanuts

1 tablespoon light soy sauce

Saucepan with a lid (for the rice)
Large wok or frying pan

• METHOD •

1 Wash the aubergine. Trim the stalk end, cut into 2-cm/¾-inch slices and cross-chop into sticks about 7 mm/⅓ inch wide. Sprinkle with fine salt and leave for 30 minutes–1 hour in a large sieve or on a plate to sweat (I do not suggest leaving it in a colander because you will need that for draining the beansprouts). Rinse under the cold tap and spread out to dry on a large plate lined with kitchen paper. Thoroughly pick over the beansprouts, wash and leave to drain in a colander.

2 Rinse the rice under the cold tap until the water runs clear and put into the saucepan with a lid. Add 600 ml/1 pint salted or unsalted water for 310 g/10 oz or 800 ml/1⅓ pints for 400 g/ 13 oz rice. Bring to the boil, stir, cover and simmer for 12 minutes for Thai rice, or 20 minutes for other types of long-grain white rice. Leave to rest, covered, for 10–15 minutes.

3 While the rice simmers, wash, dry and quarter the pepper. Cut out any dark spots and discard the core, seeds and white inner pith. Chop into sticks 5 mm/less than ¼ inch wide and 2.5cm/1 inch long. Peel the onion, slice in half across and cut into strips the same size as the pepper. Wash and top and tail the beans; cut into 2-cm/¾-inch lengths and spread on a plate lined with kitchen paper to dry. Peel and thinly slice the garlic and ginger, trimming off fibrous patches on the ginger.

4 Make the sweet-and-sour sauce. Squeeze the ½ lemon and mix 1 tablespoon of the juice with the vinegar, sugar, sherry, soy sauces, cornflour and stock or water. Beat with a fork until homogenous.

5 Do not start frying the vegetables until the rice has rested for at least 5 minutes. Check that the beans and beansprouts are dry and, if necessary, blot with kitchen paper. Set all the prepared ingredients plus the peanuts conveniently to hand near the cooker. Warm the oil over high heat in the wok or frying-pan, add the garlic and ginger and fry for 20 seconds or until just beginning to change colour (they should not be allowed to brown, as the stir-frying takes over 5 minutes and they might burn). Add the aubergine and stir-fry for 30 seconds; add the pepper and stir-fry for 1½ minutes. Add the onion and beansprouts and stir for 1 minute; add the beans and stir for 1½ minutes. Add the nuts and stir for another minute. Quickly beat up and add the sauce. Stir until it thickens and serve with the rice.

• FRIED RICE WITH • CORN AND CASHEW NUTS

This recipe, so far as I know, has no claim whatever to authenticity – but that does not make the result any less enjoyable.

The creamy taste of the cashew nuts is central to the dish: I know that they are not cheap, but pieces cost less than whole, shelled nuts (if you are prepared to buy in large quantity, you can sometimes find them at bargain prices in Oriental stores).

Fresh corn is well worth the surprisingly small amount of extra work involved in cutting off the kernels; otherwise, frozen is a better alternative than tinned, which is not only less crisp but sometimes sweetened. If it is fresh and young, corn on the cob will have a green rather than straw-like husk and pale, undeveloped kernels at the tip.

To ensure that the rice is light and dry before frying, set it to simmer at least an hour before the meal: if you like, cook it the previous day.

Serve with Red-Chilli Oil (optional).

For 3

• INGREDIENTS •

250 g/8 oz Thai fragrant or white Patna or American long-grain rice

Salt

375 g/12 oz unpodded, fresh peas or 190 g/6 oz frozen

2 fresh cobs or 190 g/6 oz frozen sweetcorn

2 sticks celery

Small bunch coriander (enough for 2 tablespoons when chopped)

150 g/5 oz (1 medium) onion

2 cloves garlic

3-cm/1¼-inch piece fresh root ginger

1 moderately hot green chilli

1½ teaspoons sugar

4 tablespoons soy sauce

90 g/3 oz unsalted cashew nuts

90 g/3 oz unsalted peanuts

75 g/2½ oz desiccated coconut

2½ tablespoons oil

Saucepan with a lid (for the rice)
Sharp knife (for cutting off fresh corn kernels)
Large wok or frying-pan
Wok-scoop or spatula (if available)

• METHOD •

1 Rinse the rice until the water runs clear, put it into the saucepan with a lid and add 500 ml/⅞ pint salted or unsalted water. Bring to the boil, stir, cover and simmer for 12 minutes for Thai or 20 minutes for other types of rice: be particularly careful not to let it overcook. Leave to rest, covered, for 45 minutes or more. If cooked in advance, loosen with a fork, allow to become completely cold and store, covered, in the refrigerator.

2 Pod the peas if necessary. Just cover with salted water and boil for 5–15 minutes if fresh or 2 minutes if frozen (the time fresh ones take depends on age and size). Remove the leaves

and silky hair from fresh corn and wash. Just cover the corn with water (do not add salt). Boil corn on the cob for 6–7 minutes or until tender; cook frozen kernels according to the instructions on the packet. Drain. Leave fresh corn until it is cool enough to handle and cut off the kernels by standing the head upright and slicing downwards with the sharp knife.

3 Cut off the leaves and trim the root ends of the celery, pare off any discoloured streaks, wash, dry and chop into 2-cm/¾-inch pieces. Then cross-chop into sticks 5 mm/less than ¼ inch wide. Trim the ends of the coriander stems; wash, shake off surplus moisture and chop coarsely. Peel and finely chop the onion. Peel and thinly slice the garlic and ginger, discarding any fibrous patches on the ginger. Wash and dry the chilli and trim the stalk end; dice as finely as possible (do not remove the seeds). Avoid touching your eyes while handling it and wash your hands afterwards.

4 Mix the sugar with the soy sauce. Put all the prepared ingredients plus the cashews, peanuts, coconut and an empty plate within reach of the cooker. Loosen the rice with a fork. Warm ½ tablespoon of the oil in the wok or frying-pan over medium heat, add the peanuts and cashew nuts and stir-fry for 30 seconds or until the cashew nuts are just starting to turn gold (do not let them colour more than very slightly, since they burn easily). Remove the pan from the heat and transfer the nuts to the plate. Wipe the wok to remove any fragments of peanut skin and warm the remaining 2 tablespoons oil over high heat. Add the garlic and ginger and allow to fry until starting to change colour. Add the celery and stir-fry for 20 seconds; add the onion and stir for 1 minute. Add the chilli and stir. Reduce the heat to medium: if your ring is electric and responds slowly to a change of setting, lift the pan for a second or two. Add the rice and stir-fry for 2 minutes using the wok-scoop or spatula (if available); make sure that all the grains are separated and no unmixed lumps remain. Stir in the peas, coconut and corn. Pour the soy sauce into the pan and stir until absorbed. Add the nuts and stir; stir in the coriander. Serve at once.

• STIR-FRIED MUSHROOMS •
AND GREEN PEPPER
WITH CELERY

This is an all-vegetable dish primarily designed to go with Tofu and Prawn Balls; however, you could also serve it with Steamed Eggs (page 80).

Make sure that the pepper is firm and glossy.

For 3–4

• INGREDIENTS •

310–400 g/10–13 oz Thai fragrant, Patna or American long-grain white rice

Salt

3 sticks celery

1 large green pepper

190 g/6 oz button mushrooms

2 cloves garlic

1.5-cm/⅔-inch piece fresh root ginger

1 teaspoon cornflour

2 teaspoons soy sauce

2 tablespoons stock (for preference) or water

2 tablespoons oil (3 if you use a frying-pan rather than a wok)

Saucepan with a lid (for the rice)
Wok or frying-pan

• METHOD •

1 Rinse the rice until the water runs clear and put into the saucepan with a lid. Add 600 ml/1 pint salted or unsalted water for 310 g/10 oz or 800 ml/1⅓ pints for 400 g/13 oz rice. Bring to the boil, stir, cover and simmer for 12 minutes for Thai rice, or 20 minutes for other types of white rice. Leave to rest, covered, for 10 minutes.

2 Trim the leaves and root ends of the celery and pare off any brownish streaks. Wash, dry with kitchen paper and cut into

2-cm/¾-inch lengths; cross-chop into matchsticks 5mm/less than ¼ inch wide. Wash, dry and quarter the pepper; discard the core, white inner pith and all the seeds and chop into sticks of about the same size as the celery. Trim the mushroom stalks; wash the mushrooms, blot dry and slice finely. Peel and thinly slice the garlic and ginger, trimming off any fibrous patches on the ginger.

3 Mix together the cornflour, soy sauce and stock or water. Set all the prepared ingredients within easy reach of the cooker. Warm the oil over high heat in the wok or frying-pan, add the garlic and ginger and allow to fry for 30 seconds or until changing colour. Add the celery and stir-fry for a few seconds; add the pepper and stir-fry for 1 minute. Add the mushrooms and stir for 1½–2 minutes. Pour in the soy and cornflour mixture, stir until it has thickened slightly and serve.

• ALMOND PULLAO WITH •
RED PEPPERS AND PEAS

This is reasonably cheap and, since there are relatively few vegetables to prepare, streamlined if not particularly quick. With the red pepper, green peas and rice coloured yellow with turmeric, it is also exceptionally decorative.

Preparation and cooking-time together are about 1¼ hours; cream gives added richness to the taste but can be replaced by yoghurt. Use Basmati rice if possible, since its nutty taste and texture adds to the character of the dish. The pepper should be hard and firm: if wrinkled, it is old.

Serve with Raita with Cucumber, Raita with Cumin (pages 28–29) or plain yoghurt.

For 3–4

• INGREDIENTS •

310 g/10 oz white or brown Basmati, Patna, or American long-grain rice

375 g/ 12 oz unpodded fresh peas or 190 g/6 oz frozen peas

50 g/2 oz raisins

About 310 g/10 oz (2 medium to largish) onions

3 cloves

3 black peppercorns

3 cloves garlic

2-cm/¾-inch piece fresh root ginger

2 fresh chillies, preferably 1 red and 1 green

2 tablespoons ghee plus 2 tablespoons oil or 4 tablespoons ghee

2.5-cm/1-inch stick cinnamon

½ teaspoon turmeric

⅔ teaspoon salt

85 ml/ 3 fl oz double cream (for preference) or thick whole-milk yoghurt

1 large red pepper

100 g/3½ oz unskinned whole almonds

50 g/2 oz unsalted peanuts

1 teaspoon garam masala (see page 21)

1 smallish lemon

Large saucepan with a lid
Wok or large frying-pan

• METHOD •

1 Rinse the rice until the water runs clear and leave to drain. Shell the peas if necessary. Set the raisins to soak in a little water, separating any which have stuck together.

2 Peel and finely slice the onions. Crush the cloves and peppercorns in a mortar. Peel and roughly chop the garlic and ginger, discarding any fibrous patches on the ginger; add to the mortar and crush to a paste. Wash and dry the chillies; trim off the stalk ends, slit and remove the inner membrane and seeds. Dice the flesh as finely as possible. Do not rub your eyes while handling them and wash your hands directly afterwards.

3 Warm 1 tablespoon of the ghee with 1 tablespoon of the oil (or 2 tablespoons ghee) in the large saucepan with the lid. Add half the sliced onion and fry over medium heat for 7–8 minutes or until an even pale brown, turning frequently, especially towards the end. Lower the heat: if the ring does not respond to a change of setting quickly, remove the pan from it for a moment or two. Add the chillies and stir; add the crushed flavourings, cinnamon, turmeric and salt and stir-fry for a few seconds. Add the cream or yoghurt and stir until absorbed. Add and stir-fry the rice until all the grains are coated with oil. Pour in 600ml/1 pint water, bring to the boil and add the peas. Stir thoroughly, adjust the heat to a simmer, cover and cook for 18 minutes for white Basmati, 20 minutes for other types of white rice, or 30 minutes for brown (all types). Leave, covered, for 5–10 minutes.

4 While the rice simmers, wash dry and quarter the red pepper; remove the seeds, white inner pith and any dark spots and cut the flesh into sticks about 2 cm/¾ inch long and 5–6 mm/¼ inch wide. Drain the raisins. Warm the rest of the oil and ghee (or the remaining 2 tablespoons ghee) over medium heat in the wok or frying-pan. Add the other half of the onion and fry for 2 minutes or until beginning to soften. Add the pepper and continue to fry, turning constantly, for 5–6 minutes or until the onion is an even light brown and the pepper is beginning to darken. Add the almonds and peanuts and stir-fry for 1 minute; stir in the raisins. Turn the rice into the wok or frying-pan, mix thoroughly but gently to avoid breaking the grains, sprinkle with the garam masala and squeeze the juice of the half lemon over the top. Serve at once with raita or yoghurt.

• FISH AND •
CHICKEN DISHES

Chicken is enormously popular in the East for the same reason as in this country – namely that it is relatively cheap and easy to raise: in fact, in China it is the traditional festive food, just as beef used to be here. Fish is also eaten whenever possible, not only in coastal areas but inland, where it is farmed in every available piece of water. However, whereas I have been constantly tempted to include more, and still more recipes for chicken, the cost of fish has meant that, sadly, I have felt obliged to limit the number of fish recipes to only three.

As steaming is a favourite method of cooking fish in both Thailand and China, this seems a good place to say that except for Steamed Eggs (page 80), I have avoided it on the assumption that readers will not have a steamer. The particular advantage of this method is that items cook gently and retain all their juices and flavour, much of which leaches into the water if they are boiled. Fish is generally steamed on the plate in which it is to be served so that none of the juices are lost and there is no danger of the fish breaking. However, as grilling or baking also preserve and, indeed, concentrate flavour you will obtain just as good, if not quite the same result, by grilling the fish whole (see Grilled Fish with Garlic and Mushrooms, opposite).

• GRILLED FISH WITH •
GARLIC AND MUSHROOMS

I suggest this as a quick, easy and not-too-expensive dish to serve with Vatch's Charred Chilli Sauce (see page 33). Just as the potency of the sauce means that only a dab of it is needed, so you also need relatively little fish (I reckon that 125–150 g/4–5 oz per person is plenty: of course you can serve more if you wish).

For 4

• INGREDIENTS •

400–450 g/13–14 oz Thai fragrant or brown or white Patna or American long-grain rice

Salt

250 g/8 oz button mushrooms

4 cloves garlic

½ small lemon

500–625 g/1–1¼ lb cod or haddock fillets

2 tablespoons oil plus a little extra

Pepper

Saucepan with a lid (for the rice)
Grill-pan or shallow ovenproof dish

• METHOD •

1 Rinse the rice under the cold tap until the water runs clear and put into the saucepan with a lid. Add 800 ml/1⅓ pints water, salted or otherwise, for 400 g/13 oz or 900 ml/1½ pints for 450 g/14 oz. Bring to the boil and stir. Cover and simmer for 12 minutes for Thai rice, 20 minutes for other types of white rice, or 30 minutes for brown. Leave to stand, covered, for at least 10 minutes.

2 Trim the ends of the mushroom stalks; wash and dry the mushrooms and slice finely. Peel and thinly slice the garlic. Squeeze the lemon. Skin the fish: pull the skin sharply from the thickest corner. If it sticks, ease it off with a knife. Wash the fish in cold water, dry with kitchen paper and check for bones.

3 Pre-heat the grill to high. If you are planning to cook in the grill-pan, take out the rack and line the pan with cooking-foil. Spread 2 tablespoons oil over the bottom (or over the bottom of the ovenproof dish) and add the slices of garlic, fairly evenly distributed. Grill for 1 minute. Arrange the mushrooms on top, season moderately with salt and pepper, and grill for 3 minutes. Turn and grill for another 3 minutes. Remove from the heat and cover with the fish: season moderately with salt and pepper again, dribble with a little oil and grill for 3–4 minutes or until the fish is opaque all through and can be flaked with a fork. Sprinkle with 2 teaspoons lemon juice and serve at once, accompanied by the rice and sauce.

• FISH PULLAO WITH COCONUT •

This pullao is based directly on Spiced Rice, with coconut milk as an additional flavouring. The sweetness of the coconut brings out the taste of the fish and gives the pullao its character.

In view of the price of fish, the recipe is fairly cheap, since you need only 375 g/12 oz for 3 or 4 people and not much else apart from rice, coriander and coconut.

The coconut milk must be made in advance (see page 24): otherwise the pullao takes only about 30 minutes to make – that is, no longer than the rice needs to simmer and rest.

Serve alone or accompanied by Shobhna's Green-Chilli Chutney (page 32).

For 3–4

• INGREDIENTS •

310 g/10 oz brown or white Patna or American long-grain rice

6 cardamom pods

3 tablespoons ghee plus 1 tablespoon oil or 2 tablespoons each ghee and oil

6 cloves

7.5-cm/3-inch stick cinnamon

½ teaspoon cumin seeds

1 teaspoon fennel seeds

Salt

300–450 ml/½–¾ pint coconut milk	½ small lemon
375 g/12 oz filleted cod or haddock	2–3 fairy mild green chillies
310 g/10 oz (2 medium) onions	50 g/2 oz grated fresh or desiccated coconut
3-cm/1¼-inch piece fresh root ginger	
Bunch coriander (enough for 2 tablespoons when chopped: optional)	

Thick-based saucepan with a lid (for the rice)
Wok or deep frying-pan

• METHOD •

1 Prepare the rice. Place in a sieve and rinse under the cold tap until the water runs clear; leave to drain. Bruise the cardamoms with a pestle and mortar so that the pods are opened; other spices can be left whole. Warm 1 tablespoon of ghee or oil in the thick-based saucepan over medium heat and add the cardamoms, cloves, cinnamon, cumin, fennel seeds and 1 teaspoon salt. Fry for a few seconds, until the cumin seeds pop, turning once or twice: stand back in case they splutter. Add the rice and stir-fry until all the grains are coated with oil and the pan is quite dry (the rinsed rice will have been wet). Pour in the coconut milk and bring to the boil. Stir thoroughly, reduce the heat to low and cook, uncovered, for 5–7 minutes or until the milk is absorbed. Add 150 ml/¼ pint boiling water, cover and simmer for 13–15 minutes for white rice or 23–25 for brown, or until just tender. Leave to rest, covered, for 10 minutes or until the other ingredients are ready.

2 While the rice cooks, skin the fish if necessary. Pull the skin firmly from the thickest corner: if it sticks, scrape it off with a knife. Wash the flesh in cold water, check for bones and divide into chunks. Peel and finely slice the onions. Peel and slice the ginger, discarding any fibrous patches; put into a mortar and crush. Trim the ends of the coriander stems, wash and blot dry and chop fairly finely. Squeeze the lemon. Wash and dry the chillies and trim the stalk ends; slit and remove the inner membrane and some of the seeds if you want the pullao to be relatively mild, then chop the flesh finely. Do not rub your

eyes while chopping and wash your hands directly afterwards. Add the coriander, chillies, 1 tablespoon lemon juice and the grated or desiccated coconut to the mortar, plus 1 tablespoon water if the coconut is desiccated. Pound to a rough paste.

3 Do not start cooking the rest of the ingredients until the rice has rested. Loosen it with a fork. Warm 3 tablespoons ghee and/or oil in the wok or deep frying-pan. Add the onions and fry over medium heat for 6–7 minutes or until pale gold but not brown, turning often, especially towards the end. Add the fish, season with ½ teaspoon salt and fry for 1–1½ minutes or until it is opaque and starting to flake; turn constantly. Add the paste from the mortar and stir-fry for 30 seconds; add the rice and stir-fry for about a minute, until thoroughly mixed. Serve at once, with Green-Chilli Chutney if you wish.

• CHICKEN WITH YOGHURT •
AND LEMON ZEST

For this dish the chicken is pricked all over so that it absorbs the flavourings with which it is simmered. It smells wonderful as it cooks: the final effect is piquant rather than hot and, because of the yoghurt, very slightly tart.

You can use any part of the chicken – breasts, legs or even drumsticks. Drumsticks and legs are cheaper and have more flavour than boned breasts but look less elegant, partly because the flesh shrinks from the bone while cooking.

For 2–3

• INGREDIENTS •

190 g/6 oz (1 medium/largish) onion	5 black peppercorns
5–6 cloves garlic	1 lemon
4 cardamom pods	Salt
4 cloves	1 green chilli

2-3 chicken legs or breasts or 4-6 drumsticks	*250–375 g/8–12 oz white Basmati, Patna or American long grain rice*
3 tablespoons ghee or 2 tablespoons ghee plus 1 tablespoon oil	*150 g/5 oz (1 small carton) whole-milk yoghurt*
2.5-cm/1-inch stick cinnamon	*1 teaspoon garam masala (see page 21)*

Grater
Wok or largish saucepan with a lid
Smaller saucepan with a lid (for the rice)
Egg-whisk

• METHOD •

1 Peel and finely slice the onion. Peel and roughly chop the garlic. Bruise the cardamoms in a mortar so that the pods are open. Remove from the mortar and replace with the cloves and peppercorns. Crush the cloves and peppercorns; then add and crush the garlic. Wash and dry the lemon and finely grate the zest (the yellow part of the skin); add with 1 teaspoon salt to the flavourings in the mortar. Wash and dry the chilli and cut off the stalk end; slit, remove all or some of the seeds and inner membrane if you wish, and dice the flesh as finely as possible. Do not rub your eyes while chopping it and wash your hands afterwards.

2 Skin the chicken if necessary: pull the skin from the flesh sharply, starting at the thickest corner. With legs, you may be able to detach it by pulling it over the bone end, but if you cannot, use a knife or scissors. Wash thoroughly in cold water, remove any fat which remains on the flesh and prick all over with a kitchen knife or skewer. Wash your hands and the utensils.

3 Warm the ghee (or ghee and oil) in the wok or saucepan over medium heat and add the onion. Fry for 5–6 minutes or until an even pale gold, turning constantly, particularly towards the end (a wok is helpful in that any pieces which become too coloured can be pushed up the side). Add the chicken and turn in the oil for 1 minute or until white all over. Lower the heat or remove the pan from the ring for a moment or two (it is vital not to burn the flavourings) and add the chilli, the contents of the mortar and the cinnamon (whole). Turn in the oil and add 600 ml/1 pint water. Bring to the boil, cover and cook at a fast simmer (so that the water is just bubbling) for 35–40 minutes or until the chicken is tender and no pink liquid emerges when it is pierced with a knife.

4 Set the rice to cook when the chicken has been simmering for 15 minutes. Rinse until the water runs clear, put into the smaller saucepan with a lid and add 500–750 ml/⅞–1¼ pints salted or unsalted water, depending on the quantity of rice. Bring to the boil, stir, cover and simmer for 18 minutes for Basmati or 20 minutes for other types of white rice. Leave to rest, covered, until the chicken is ready.

5 Whisk the yoghurt until completely smooth and homogenous and set within easy reach of the cooker; also put a plate conveniently to hand. When the chicken is tender, raise the heat to high and cook until the liquid has evaporated, leaving the onions and flavourings as a thick sauce. Reduce the heat to medium/low and transfer the pieces of chicken from the pan to the plate. Incorporate the yoghurt into the sauce gradually: add 1 tablespoon at a time, stir gently and allow the sauce to reduce slightly before adding the next. When all the yoghurt has been added, allow the sauce to cook until it is again thick and reduced to about 6 tablespoons. Return the chicken to the pan and toss in the sauce to reheat. Sprinkle with the garam masala and serve with the rice.

• SHEHZAD'S TANDOORI-STYLE • CHICKEN

I particularly recommend this for parties because it entails relatively little work and the marinade has to be made in advance, which leaves plenty of time for other preparations. (The quantities below are for only 2 but can be increased as necessary.)

You cannot achieve an authentic result without a proper tandoori oven, which is a tall, beehive-shaped structure heated from underneath by charcoal: to approximate it as closely as possible, Shehzad suggests baking at high heat and drying the oven by turning it on 30 minutes before putting in the chicken, which is heavy on fuel. Instead, you can simply heat the oven to high and bake the chicken at high or moderate heat, as you prefer. Alternatively grilling gives excellent flavour: particularly with the grill, however, you must watch carefully and baste fairly frequently.

Serve with Raita with Cucumbner and Mint (page 29) or plain, Spinach or Spiced Rice (pages 39–40).

For 2

• INGREDIENTS •

2 chicken quarters	1 teaspoon salt
3 cloves garlic	150 g/5 oz whole-milk yoghurt
1.5-cm/⅗-inch piece fresh root ginger	2 tablespoons oil
1 small or ½ large lemon	250 g/8 oz Spiced Rice (see page39), Spinach Rice (page 40) or white or brown Basmati, Patna or American long-grain rice
1 teaspoon garam masala (see page 21)	
1 teaspoon hot chilli powder	

Saucepan with a lid (for the rice)
Grill-pan or baking dish

• METHOD •

1 Skin the chicken: pull the skin sharply from the thickest corner; if you cannot detach it by pulling it over the bone at the end of the leg, use a knife or scissors. Remove any fat which clings to the flesh and wash thoroughly in cold water. Dry with kitchen paper and slash in four or five places so that the flavour of the marinade will permeate the meat. Wash your hands and the utensils.

2 Peel and roughly slice the garlic and ginger, removing any fibrous patches on the ginger; thoroughly crush in a mortar. Squeeze the lemon. Mix the crushed garlic and ginger, garam masala, chilli powder and salt with the yoghurt, oil and 2

tablespoons lemon juice to make a smooth, creamy paste. Set the chicken in it, spooning it all over the meat. You will find that there is more than perhaps you think you will need; most of the surplus, however, will be used for basting. Cover and leave to marinate for at least 3 hours; if you leave it overnight, put it at once (covered) into the refrigerator.

3 To bake the chicken by Shehzad's method, first set the oven to its highest heat. Start cooking white rice just before, or brown 10 minutes before putting in the chicken. For Spiced Rice, see page 39, or Spinach Rice, page 40; for plain rice, rinse the rice until the water runs clear, put into the saucepan with a lid, add 500ml/⅚ pint salted or unsalted water and bring to the boil. Stir, cover and cook for 18 minutes for white Basmati, 20 minutes for other types of white rice, or 30 minutes for all types of brown. Leave to rest, covered, until the chicken is ready. Line the baking-dish with cooking-foil, lay the chicken in it with its coating of marinade and bake in the oven for 25–30 minutes or until no pink liquid emerges when you insert a knife into the bone in the thickest part. It is essential to keep an eye on it and baste at intervals: spread a spoonful of the uncooked marinade over it every 7–8 minutes or as soon as the crust starts to blacken. Serve with the rice.

To cook the chicken at a lower heat, pre-heat the oven to its highest temperature, put in the chicken when it is fully heated and then turn down the temperature to 200°C/400°F/Gas Mark 6; baste about every 10 minutes. Cooked this way, the chicken will have a deliciously crisp, golden crust. As it will take about 40 minutes, set brown rice to simmer just before you put it in and white a few minutes afterwards; leave to rest, covered, until the chicken is ready to serve.

To grill, pre-heat the grill to medium, put the chicken in a baking-dish as before, and grill for 30 minutes or until no pink liquid emerges when it is pierced. Baste every 5 minutes or as soon as the crust starts to blacken; turn at least once. Set brown rice to cook 10 minutes before starting to cook the chicken or white just before, as with Shehzad's method.

• SWEET-AND-SOUR • CHICKEN WITH CELERY AND CASHEW NUTS

With this dish it is particularly important not to overfry the vegetables, which should retain all their crispness and freshness. The only exception to this is the garlic, which adds a balancing sharpness to the flavour if well browned.

I have suggested using chicken breasts rather than legs because they are easier to cut up, although dearer and with less flavour.

The chicken is coated with an egg white; the yolk is not needed, but you can use it in scrambled eggs or omelettes. It can be kept for up to 24 hours (covered) in the refrigerator.

For 3–4

• INGREDIENTS •

190 g/6 oz (1 medium or 2 small) courgettes

Salt, some of which should be finely ground

310–400 g/10–13 oz Thai fragrant, Patna or American long-grain white rice

2 boned chicken breasts weighing about 250 g/8 oz together

½ lemon

1 tablespoon white-wine vinegar

25 g/1 oz (1 tablespoon) white sugar

25 g/1 oz (1 tablespoon) soft dark-brown sugar

2 tablespoons medium-dry sherry

2 tablespoons soy sauce

3 tablespoons chicken stock or water

3 level teaspoons cornflour

1 egg (white only)

3 sticks celery

50 g/2oz mange-tout peas

2 large or 3 small cloves garlic

2.5-cm/1-inch piece fresh root ginger

50g/2 oz cashew nuts

4 tablespoons oil

Sharp knife
Saucepan with a lid (for the rice)
Wok or frying-pan

• METHOD •

1 Wash the courgette(s) and trim the ends. Cut into 2-cm/¾-inch slices and cross-chop into sticks 5 mm/less than ¼ inch wide. Sprinkle with fine salt and leave to sweat in a sieve or colander for 30–45 minutes. Rinse under the cold tap and spread out on a plate lined with kitchen paper to dry.

2 Unless the rice you are using is Thai fragrant, set the rice to simmer: as Thai rice takes only 10–12 minutes, do not start cooking it until after you have cut up the chicken. Rinse under the cold tap until the water runs clear, put into the saucepan with a lid and add 600 ml/1 pint salted or unsalted water for 310 g/10 oz or 800 ml/1⅓ pints for 400 g/13 oz rice. Bring to the boil, stir, cover and simmer for 12 minutes for Thai rice or 20 minutes for other types of rice. Leave to rest, covered, for 30 minutes or until the sauce is ready.

3 Skin the chicken if necessary: pull the skin sharply from the thickest corner. Remove any fat which clings to the flesh, wash thoroughly in cold water and spread out flat on a chopping surface or large plate. Using the sharp knife, cut into strips 7mm/⅓ inch wide and 2.5 cm/1 inch long. Wash your hands and the utensils.

4 Make the sweet-and-sour sauce. Squeeze the ½ lemon and mix together 1 tablespoon of the juice, the vinegar, sugars, sherry, soy sauce and stock or water. Add 1 tablespoon to the chicken; toss to mix thoroughly. Sprinkle 1 teaspoon of the cornflour over the meat and toss to mix again; beat the remaining 2 teaspoons cornflour into the sauce. Separate the egg: crack sharply in the middle and break over a small bowl, holding it at an angle so that the yolk does not escape. Tip the yolk from one half of the shell to the other until all the white has fallen out. Beat the white briefly with a fork, pour over the chicken and toss to mix for a third time. Leave the meat to marinate while you prepare the rest of the ingredients. Wash up the bowl and fork used for the egg white (for health reasons it is a good idea to wash implements used for raw egg as soon as they have been used).

5 Trim the root and leaf ends of the celery, scrape off any discoloured patches, wash and dry. Cut into 2-cm/¾-inch slices; then cross-chop into sticks 5mm/less than ¼ inch wide. Trim the ends of the peas, wash and cut into diagonal slices 1 cm/½ inch wide. Peel and thinly slice the garlic and ginger, removing any fibrous patches on the ginger.

6 Check that the peas and courgettes are dry. Place all the prepared ingredients plus the cashew nuts within easy reach of the cooker; you should also set 2 empty plates to hand. Warm 2 tablespoons of the oil in the wok or frying-pan over medium heat. Add half the garlic and ginger and allow to fry for 30-40 seconds or until pale brown. Add the nuts and stir-fry until they start to turn gold: watch carefully, since they burn easily. Transfer, with the garlic and ginger, to one of the empty plates. Raise the heat slightly and add the chicken to the pan; stir-fry for 2–2½ minutes, until opaque and just starting to colour; place on the second plate. Take the pan from the heat and wipe it clean with kitchen paper. Raise the heat to high, return the pan and warm the remaining 2 tablespoons oil. Add the rest of the garlic and ginger and fry until gold. Add the celery and stir-fry for 30 seconds; add the courgette(s) and stir for another 30 seconds. Add the peas and stir for 1½–2 minutes. Return the chicken to the pan, stir briefly and pour in the sauce. Cook until it thickens; stir in the nuts and serve with the rice.

• SHEHZAD'S CHICKEN •
PULLAO WITH LEMON

Like several of the other recipes which Shehzad has contributed, this is discreetly flavoured and very simple.

Shehzad suggests using a chicken leg and a breast, but I advise 2 boned breasts because, although dearer and with less flavour than legs, they are very much easier to cut up. However you can use a leg, or two legs (which will not be boned) if you prefer: directions for boning and chopping them are given below. Make sure that the chicken is fresh.

Serve with Raita with Cucumber (see page 28).

For 3–4

• INGREDIENTS •

2 boned chicken breasts weighing 250–310 g/8–10 oz in total, or 2 chicken legs weighing 310–450 g/10–14 oz in total, or 1 chicken breast and 1 chicken leg

250 g/8 oz unpodded fresh or 125 g/ 4 oz frozen peas

190 g/6 oz (1 medium to largish) onion

2 medium-sized ripe tomatoes

1 teaspoon coriander seeds

4–5 small cloves garlic

1 small or ½ large lemon

375 g/12 oz white Basmati, Patna or American long-grain rice

4 tablespoons oil

1 bayleaf

1 teaspoon hot chilli powder

1½ teaspoons salt

Sharp, preferably smallish knife (for boning and chopping chicken legs)
Wok or large saucepan with a lid

• METHOD •

1 Skin the chicken: pull the skin sharply from the thickest corner. If you cannot detach it from the bone end of the legs, use a knife or scissors. Wash the pieces thoroughly in cold water and dry with kitchen paper. Cut the flesh from around the bone of the legs as closely as possible, using the sharp knife. Chop the meat into cubes about 1 × 1.5 cm/½ × ⅔ inch. With leg meat, cut along the grain and cross-chop: do not worry if you cannot sever string-like membranes or if the pieces are not very neatly shaped (breast meat can be cut whichever way is most convenient). Wash your hands and the utensils.

2 Pod the peas if necessary. Peel and finely slice the onion. Skin the tomatoes (see page 31, step 2) and chop the flesh fairly finely, discarding the hard cores. Crush the coriander in a mortar; peel, roughly chop and crush the garlic. Squeeze the

lemon and reserve the juice. Rinse the rice under the cold tap until the water runs clear and leave to drain in a sieve.

3 Warm the oil in the wok or large saucepan over medium heat and fry the onions for 7–8 minutes or until an even pale brown, turning constantly, especially after they have begun to change colour. Add the bayleaf and stir. Lower the heat: if you have an electric ring which takes time to cool, remove the pan from the heat for a moment or two. Add the crushed garlic and coriander, chilli powder, salt, tomatoes, 2 tablespoons lemon juice and the peas and cook for about 2 minutes, stirring continuously. Add the chicken and continue to cook, still stirring continuously, for another 2 minutes. Add the rice, stir thoroughly so that all the grains are coated with flavouring and oil, and add 750ml/1¼ pints water. Bring to the boil and stir again. Lower the heat to a simmer, cover and cook for 18 minutes for Basmati or 20 minutes for other types of rice. Leave to rest, covered, for 5–10 minutes before serving with the chicken.

• FRIED RICE WITH •
LEFT-OVER CHICKEN
AND PRAWNS

Originally this recipe was intended to be merely a way of using up the chicken left over from making stock. As it has turned out, however, this by no means does it justice: it might perhaps be better to say that you can make stock as a by-product of the meat.

Although the chicken must be thoroughly cooked through, it is important not to overcook it; also, to prevent it from drying out, you should use it as soon as possible after it is boned. As the rice has to be set to simmer about an hour before the meal, I suggest starting to cook the chicken when the rice is taken from the heat (if you like, however, you can simmer the rice several hours or even a day in advance, in which case allow the chicken 45–50 minutes).

Simmering the rice in advance gives it time to dry out before frying: if you fry it while it is still moist, it will be heavy and soggy rather than light and dry.

If possible, use fresh rather than frozen prawns: prawns which are sold unshelled will have more flavour than shelled. Remember that frozen ones will take several hours to defrost.

For 3, or 4 at a pinch

• INGREDIENTS •

310 g/10 oz Thai fragrant or white Patna or American long-grain rice

Salt

2 chicken legs

250 g/8 oz unshelled or 125g/4oz shelled prawns

90 g/3 oz Kenya or other fine, stringless, green beans

1 large green pepper

150 g/5 oz button mushrooms

125 g/4 oz (1 small to medium) onion

2 cloves garlic

1 stick lemon grass

1 moderately hot green chilli

½ lemon

3 tablespoons fish sauce

2 tablespoons oil

2 saucepans with lids (for the rice and chicken)
Large wok or frying-pan
Wok-scoop or spatula (if available)

• METHOD •

1 Rinse the rice under the cold tap until the water runs clear and put into the saucepan with a lid. Add 600 ml/1 pint water, plus salt if you wish, stir, cover and simmer for 12 minutes for Thai rice or 20 minutes for other types of rice. Leave to rest, covered, for at least 45 minutes.

2 Make the chicken stock following the instructions on page 25. Chop the cooked meat as neatly as you can into strips about 2.5 cm/1 inch long and 1 cm/½ inch wide.

3 Shell the prawns if necessary: pull off the head of each one and the shell from the tail; pick off the rest of the shell over the body. Wash in cold water and leave in a sieve to drain. Wash and drain ready-shelled prawns; drain frozen ones.

4 Top and tail and wash the beans; cut into 2-cm/¾-inch lengths and spread on a plate lined with kitchen paper to dry. Wash, dry and quarter the pepper. Discard the core and seeds, trim off the white inner pith and cut the flesh into strips 2.5 cm/1 inch long and 5–6 mm/¼ inch wide. Trim the mushroom stalks and wash and dry the mushrooms; slice finely. Peel and finely chop the onion; peel and slice the garlic. Cut off the leaves and trim the root of the lemon grass, peel off the outer layer and slice finely. Wash and dry the chilli; trim the stalk end and finely chop (do not remove the seeds). Avoid rubbing your eyes while handling it and wash your hands afterwards. Put the garlic, lemon grass, chilli and ½ teaspoon salt into a mortar and crush to a rough paste.

5 Squeeze the lemon. Loosen the rice with a fork so that it can be turned easily into the pan. Put all the prepared ingredients plus the fish sauce within easy reach of the cooker. Warm the oil in the wok or frying-pan over high heat. Add the beans and stir-fry for 20 seconds; add the onion and stir-fry for another 20 seconds. Add the pepper and stir for 1 minute; add the mushrooms and stir for another minute. Add the paste and stir. Lower the heat to medium: if you have an electric ring which responds slowly to a change of setting, remove the pan from the heat for a second or two. Add the rice and stir for 2 minutes, using the wok-scoop or spatula (if available); take care to ensure that every grain is separate and all parts of it thoroughly mixed. Add the prawns and chicken and stir; add the fish sauce and 1 tablespoon lemon juice, stir until absorbed and serve.

· MEAT DISHES ·

The belief in the sacred cow in India means that many Indians do not eat beef; however, the Indian cookery-writer Shehzad Hussein has contributed a recipe for minced beef (see page 126). Similarly, in China shortage of suitable grazing and the widespread use of oxen for farmwork has meant that beef has always been a rarity, although Yan-kit So favours it. Lamb is, to a large extent, a substitute for beef in India; in Thailand and China it is replaced by pork, which is used in a huge variety of ways, notably for stir-fries and to put into soups. As it has turned out, there is only one pork dish in this chapter: the rest have been put elsewhere in the book (see Pork with Oyster Sauce and Kohlrabi in the dinner-parties chapter, page 158, Thai-style Pork with Eggs, page 82 and Pork Slivers and Mushrooms in Broth with Star Anise, page 52. My inclusion of several Chinese-style beef dishes is simply for the sake of variety, since in the previous books I have given no recipes for beef at all except for hamburgers and Bolognese sauce to go with pasta. Neither of the beef dishes in this chapter is expensive: for one (Stir-fried Beef with Swede and Spinach, page 128) you need only a little rump or minute steak, and for the other (Shehzad's Hot Spiced Beef with Vegetables, page 126) a surprisingly modest amount of minced beef.

• PEPPERMINT LAMB •

The inspiration for this dish was the powerful but irresistible smell of fresh mint drifting across the pavement from a Greek grocer's shop. In view of the British custom of serving mint sauce with lamb, teaming the herb with lamb seemed obvious.

I have given quantities for 3 because this amount of meat is about half that on an average-sized half-leg. Leg is the only cut which yields suitably lean meat, and is expensive; however, you can use the rest for Shehzad's Lamb with Lemon and Tomatoes (page 120), or Lamb Pullao (page 121), which means that it will stretch to 6 or 7 servings. If you want to make one of the first two, buy an upper (fillet) half; for pullao, choose the lower (knuckle) end, which carries more bone and will make a richer stock. You can ask a butcher to bone the meat, trim off the fat and cut the lean meat into 2-cm/¾-inch squares; directions for boning and chopping it yourself, however, are given below. (If you plan to make pullao and ask a butcher to cut the meat from a knuckle half, make sure that the bone is severed at the lower end so that it will fit into a saucepan.)

Mint, like basil, wilts quickly. Either put it in water as soon as possible and use it on the same day or store it for up to 24 hours in an airtight bag in the refrigerator.

Use real Greek, as opposed to Greek-style, yoghurt (real Greek yoghurt is very mild and will not curdle).

The total cooking time is about 1 hour 40 minutes.

For 3

• INGREDIENTS •

500–625 g/1–1¼ lb lamb (boned weight)

310 g/10 oz (2 medium) onions

5 cloves

6 black peppercorns

5 cloves garlic

2.5-cm/1-inch piece fresh root ginger

2 green chillies

1 tablespoon oil

2 tablespoons ghee

1 *teaspoon ground turmeric*

1 *teaspoon yellow mustard seeds*

3-cm/1¼-inch *stick cinnamon*

Salt

310–375 g/10–12 oz *Basmati, Patna*
or American long-grain rice

3–4 *good-sized spears mint (enough*
for 2 tablespoons when chopped)

½ *small lemon*

150 g/5 oz *Greek yoghurt*

Sharp knife (for cutting up the lamb)
Wok or large saucepan or frying-pan with a lid
Saucepan with a lid (for the rice)

• METHOD •

1 Prepare the meat. If it is already chopped, wash it in cold water, blot dry with kitchen paper and remove any remaining visible fat. If it is not chopped, wash it and place on a chopping-board or other suitable surface: if you have nowhere else, cut it up in the sink. With a fillet half, cut the meat down to the bone into 2-cm/¾-inch slices using the sharp knife; sever it from the bone after slicing, cutting as close to the bone as you can. With a knuckle half, cut and sever 2 slices from the thick end and remove the rest of the meat from the bone in one piece. A little will be left at the top on the side from which you did not cut the slices: leave this, and other remnants, for pullao. Weigh the meat: put the part that you do not need on a plate, cover with foodwrap and store in the refrigerator. With a knuckle half, use the 2 steaks plus a little more from the remaining chunk of meat (the steaks are easier to chop tidily than the meat from lower down, and untidier pieces do not matter for pullao). Trim all the fat from the meat to be used immediately and cut into 2-cm/¾-inch squares.

2 Peel and finely slice the onions. Crush the cloves and peppercorns in a mortar. Peel and roughly chop the garlic and ginger, discarding any fibrous patches on the ginger; add to the mortar and crush to a paste. Wash and dry the chillies and trim the stalk ends; slit, remove the inner membrane and all or some of the seeds and dice the flesh as finely as possible. Do not rub your eyes while handling them and wash your hands directly afterwards.

3 Warm the oil and ghee over medium heat in the wok or pan with a lid. Add the onions and fry for 6–7 minutes or until lightly but evenly coloured; turn constantly, especially towards the end. Add the lamb and stir-fry until pale but not deep brown on all sides. Reduce the heat to low: with an electric ring which cools slowly, remove the pan from the heat for a moment or two. Add the chillies and stir; add the crushed flavourings, turmeric, mustard seeds and cinnamon (whole) plus 1 teaspoon salt and turn in the oil for a few seconds. Pour in 600 ml/1 pint water, bring to the boil, stir and simmer, covered, for 1¼ hours or until the lamb is tender.

4 If using brown rice, set it to cook when the lamb has been simmering for 40–45 minutes; if using white rice, set it to cook after 50–55 minutes. Rinse under the cold tap until the water runs clear, put into the saucepan with a lid, add 600 ml/ 1 pint salted or unsalted water for 310 g/10 oz rice or 750 ml/ 1¼ pints for 375 g/12 oz; bring to the boil. Stir, cover and simmer for 18 minutes for white Basmati, 20 minutes for other types of white rice, or 30 minutes for all types of brown. Leave to rest, covered, until the lamb is ready.

5 Wash the mint; pull the leaves from the stems and chop the leaves finely. Squeeze 2 teaspoons lemon juice. When the lamb is tender, uncover, raise the heat to medium and boil, stirring often, until the liquid in the pan is thick and reduced to about 6 tablespoons: this will take 7–10 minutes. Stir in the mint and yoghurt and continue to cook for 3 minutes or until the sauce is deep greenish-gold and again slightly reduced; turn constantly. Remove from the heat, stir in the lemon juice and serve with the rice.

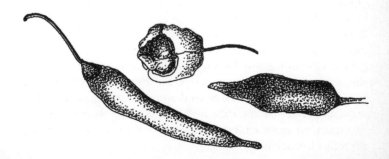

· Shehzad's Lamb with · Lemon and Tomatoes

This is not dramatically spicy but a remarkably effective way of bringing out the rich flavour of lamb.

Use half the meat from a fillet half or knuckle end of leg: for boning it see page 118.

For 3–4

· INGREDIENTS ·

500–625 g/1–1¼ lb meat from a half-leg of lamb

500g/1 lb ripe tomatoes

250 g/8 oz (2 medium to small) onions

2.5-cm/1-inch piece fresh root ginger

4 cloves garlic

1 hot green chilli

4 tablespoons oil

⅔ teaspoon soft dark-brown or white sugar

Salt

1 tablespoon tomato purée

310–375 g/10–12 oz brown or white Basmati, Patna or American long-grain rice

Few sprigs coriander (optional)

½ large or 1 small lemon

Wok or largish saucepan with a lid
Saucepan with a lid (for the rice)

· METHOD ·

1 Wash the meat and blot dry with kitchen paper. Trim off all the fat and cut into 1.5 × 2cm/⅔ × ¾ inch cubes.

2 Peel the tomatoes (see page 31) and chop fairly finely, discarding the hard cores. Peel and finely slice the onions; peel and chop the ginger and garlic, discarding any fibrous patches on the ginger. Wash and dry the chilli and trim the stalk end; dice finely (do not remove the seeds). Avoid rubbing your eyes while chopping it and wash your hands afterwards. Crush the garlic, ginger and chilli in a mortar.

3 Warm the oil over a medium heat in the wok or largish saucepan and fry the onions for 7–8 minutes or until pale brown, turning constantly, especially towards the end. Add the lamb and stir-fry for 3 minutes or until pale and opaque on all sides. Add the crushed flavourings, sugar, 1 teaspoon salt and the tomatoes and cook for 5 minutes or until the tomato flesh is liquefied, stirring constantly. Stir in the tomato purée, add 600 ml/1 pint water and bring to the boil. Cover and simmer for 50 minutes–1 hour or until the lamb is tender.

4 While the lamb simmers, cook the rice. Rinse under the cold tap until the water runs clear and put into the saucepan with a lid. Add 600 ml/1 pint water for 310 g/10 oz or 750 ml/1¼ pints for 375 g/12 oz rice, plus a little salt if you wish. Bring to the boil, stir, cover and simmer for 18 minutes for white Basmati, 20 minutes for other types of white rice or 30 minutes for brown. Leave to stand, covered, for 10 minutes.

5 Trim the coriander stems; wash, dry and chop. Squeeze 1 tablespoon lemon juice. When the lamb is tender, raise the heat and boil for 10 minutes or until the sauce is thick and reduced; stirring continuously. Add the lemon juice, sprinkle with the coriander and serve with the rice.

• LAMB PULLAO •

This is highly spiced rather than hot, although you can make it hotter by including the chilli seeds. And, yes, it is worth the trouble of making stock, which is hardly any trouble at all except that you have to be around while it simmers (which takes 2½ hours). Once the stock is skimmed and ready, you should be able to have it on the table in about 45 minutes.

The pullao is based on about half the meat plus stock made from the bone of a knuckle half leg of lamb. I suggest making the stock when you bone and cut up the meat (see page 118) and using it for this recipe the next day: it will then have time to become cold so that you can skim the fat from the top.

Serve with Raita with Cucumber or Cumin (pages 28–29) and/or Tomato Chutney with Red Pepper (page 30).

For 4

• INGREDIENTS •

STOCK

1 largish carrot

1 small onion

1 red chilli (fresh or dried)

1 bayleaf

Bone from knuckle half leg of lamb

2.5-cm/1-inch piece fresh root ginger

250–350 g/8–11 oz meat from the leg of lamb

4 black peppercorns

Salt

PULLAO

310 g/10 oz brown or white Basmati, Patna or American long-grain rice

75 g/2½ oz Kenya, French or other stringless, green beans

8 black peppercorns

6 cloves

6 cardamom pods

2 tablespoons ghee

1 level teaspoon fennel seeds

5-cm/2-inch stick cinnamon

½ teaspoon ground turmeric

⅔ teaspoon salt

75g/2½ oz raisins

250–350 g/8–11 oz lamb cooked with the stock (see below)

About 310 g/10 oz (2 medium/largish) onions

3 cloves garlic

2 red chillies

1½ tablespoons oil

90–100 g/3–3½ oz whole almonds

Large saucepan with a lid
Large wok or deep frying-pan
Wok-scoop or wooden spoon

• METHOD •

1 First make the stock. Peel and thickly slice the carrot; peel and quarter the onion. Bruise the ginger with a pestle; wash the chilli and bayleaf. Put all the prepared ingredients plus the lamb and bone into the large saucepan with a lid. (See the recipe for Peppermint Lamb on page 117 for boning the meat. Do not chop up the lamb.) Add the peppercorns, a moderate pinch of salt and 900ml–1 litre/1½–1¾ pints water or enough to cover the bone. Bring to the boil, lower the heat and skim; cover and simmer for 2½ hours or until the meat is tender and the pieces remaining on the bone can easily be detached with a blunt knife.

2 Pour the stock through a sieve into a bowl. Leave the contents of the sieve until they are cool enough to handle. Strip all the meat from the bone, discarding fat and gristle, and put with the rest of the meat on a plate. Leave to become cold, cover with foodwrap and store in the refrigerator. Throw away the bones and vegetables. Cover the stock with a plate until cold and keep until the next day either in the refrigerator or a cool place. When you are ready to use the stock, skim off the fat, which will have solidified into a solid layer over the top. Some sorts of fat, such as duck or pork fat, are excellent for certain purposes (clarified pork fat, for instance, is lard): lamb fat, however, should be thrown away.

3 When you are ready to cook the pullao, rinse the rice under the cold tap until the water runs clear. Wash the beans and chop into 1-cm/½-inch lengths. Crush the peppercorns and cloves in a mortar; bruise the cardamoms so that the pods are open (the seeds can be left intact).

4 Melt 1 tablespoon of the ghee in the saucepan with a lid over medium heat and add the crushed cloves and peppercorns, the bruised cardamoms, the fennel seeds and cinnamon (both whole), and the turmeric and salt. Stir-fry for 30 seconds or until the spices smell strongly; do not, however, allow the fennel seeds to blacken. Add the rice and stir-fry for 1½–2 minutes, until all the grains are coated with oil and the pan quite dry (the rinsed rice will have been wet). Add 600 ml/1 pint of the stock and the beans, bring to the boil and stir. Cover and simmer for 18 minutes for white Basmati, 20 minutes for other types of white rice, or 30 minutes for all types of brown. Leave to rest, covered for 10–15 minutes.

5 While the rice simmers, prepare the remaining ingredients. Set the raisins to soak in a little water. Cut the cooked meat into 2-cm/¾-inch pieces. Peel and finely slice the onions; peel and finely chop the garlic. Wash and dry the chillies and trim the stalk ends; slit, remove the inner membranes and some or all of the seeds and dice the flesh as finely as possible. Do not rub your eyes while chopping and wash your hands directly afterwards.

6 Wait until the rice is cooked before continuing. Drain the raisins. Put the rest of the ghee and the oil into the wok or deep frying-pan over medium heat and fry the onions for 4–5 minutes or until starting to change colour, turning often. Add the garlic and fry for 2 minutes or until the onions are gold but not brown; turn constantly. Stir in the chillies; add the almonds and stir-fry for 1½ minutes. Add the meat and stir-fry for 1 minute; stir in the raisins. Turn the rice into the pan and mix thoroughly but gently with the wok-scoop or wooden spoon: try not to break the grains. Remove from the heat and serve at once.

• THAI-STYLE PORK •
WITH GREEN PEPPER
AND CHILLI

This is basic, straightforward and fairly quick. The other ingredients can be prepared while the rice cooks and rests; cooking time is less than 5 minutes. With one moderately strong chilli it will be hot enough to sting but not to cloak the fresh taste of the green pepper, which is emphasized by the saltiness of the sauce. Make sure that the pepper is smooth and firm.

As the pork must be trimmed of all fat, use loin chops, which have a large area of solid lean meat.

For 3

• INGREDIENTS •

310 g/10 oz Thai fragrant or white Patna or American long-grain rice	2 pork chops weighing 375–450 g /12–14 oz in total
Salt	125 g/4 oz button mushrooms

1 large green pepper	6 black peppercorns
125 g/4 oz (1 medium to small) onion	½ teaspoon coriander seeds
	½ teaspoon sugar
2 cloves garlic	2 tablespoons fish sauce
1-cm/½-inch piece fresh root ginger	3 tablespoons oil
1 moderately hot green chilli (or 2 mild ones)	

Saucepan with a lid (for the rice)
Sharp knife
Wok or frying-pan

• METHOD •

1 Rinse the rice under the cold tap until the water runs clear and put into the saucepan with a lid. Add 600 ml/1 pint water, salted or not as you wish, and bring to the boil. Stir, cover and simmer for 12 minutes for Thai or 20 minutes for other types of rice. Leave to stand, covered, for at least 10 minutes.

2 Wash and dry the chops. Using the sharp knife, cut away the bones, fat and any tough white membranes which divide the meat. Chop into strips 2.5 cm/1 inch long and 5–6 mm/¼ inch wide; then lay each strip, which will be the thickness of the chop, on its side and halve lengthways.

3 Trim the ends of the mushroom stalks; wash, dry and slice the mushrooms very thinly. Wash and dry the pepper; cut into quarters, remove the core, seeds and white inner pith and cut the flesh into strips 2.5cm/1 inch long and 5–6 mm/¼ inch wide. Peel and finely chop the onion. Peel and finely slice the garlic and ginger, rejecting any fibrous patches on the ginger. Wash and dry the chilli and trim the stalk end; dice as finely as possible. Do not remove any seeds unless you think that it is very hot, in which case discard a few. Avoid rubbing your eyes while chopping it and wash your hands afterwards.

4 Put the peppercorns and coriander seeds into a mortar and crush. Add the garlic, ginger, chilli, sugar and 1 teaspoon salt and crush to a rough paste.

5 Place all the prepared ingredients, plus the fish sauce and a little water, within easy reach of the cooker. Measure the oil into the wok or frying-pan and set over high heat until just beginning to smoke. Add the onion and stir-fry for 20 seconds; add the pepper and stir fry for 40–50 seconds. Add the pork and stir until it is pale and opaque on all sides; add the mushrooms and stir for 40 seconds–1 minute. Add the paste and stir for a few seconds. Add the fish sauce plus 1 tablespoon water, stir briefly and serve at once with the rice.

• SHEHZAD'S HOT SPICED •
BEEF WITH VEGETABLES

This recipe is a masterpiece of economy: 250 g/8 oz minced beef, plus tomatoes, a few peas, one or two carrots, an onion and a potato (plus spices) add up to a full-flavoured curry-type dish which is ample for 4. It is fairly quick to prepare and cook, and moderately hot: serve with plain rice and Tomato Chutney with Red Pepper (page 30).

If possible, choose a waxy potato, such as Maris Bard: a floury one may disintegrate into the sauce.

The dish loses its zest and flavour if kept overnight.

For 4

• INGREDIENTS •

500 g/1 lb ripe tomatoes or 400 g/ 14 oz tin tomatoes

190 g/6 oz (1 medium/largish) onion

190 g/6 oz (1 medium) waxy potato

125–150 g/4–5 oz (1 or 2) carrots

250 g/8 oz unpodded fresh or 125g/4oz frozen peas

3 cloves garlic

2.5-cm/1-inch piece fresh root ginger

1 teaspoon salt

1 teaspoon hot chilli powder

½ teaspoon soft dark-brown sugar (if using fresh tomatoes)

1 *teaspoon garam masala (see page 21)*

1 *scant tablespoon tomato purée (if using fresh tomatoes)*

3 *tablespoons oil*

250 *g/8 oz lean minced beef*

450 *g/14 oz brown or white Patna, American long-grain or Basmati rice*

Wok or frying-pan
Saucepan with a lid (for the rice)

• METHOD •

1 If using fresh tomatoes, skin them (see page 31) and chop finely. Peel and finely slice the onion; peel the potato and carrots and cut into 5-mm/less than ¼-inch dice. Pod the peas if necessary. Peel and roughly slice the garlic and ginger, discarding any tough, fibrous patches on the ginger; crush to a paste in a mortar.

2 Mix the crushed garlic and ginger, salt, chilli powder, sugar and garam masala with the tomatoes. Warm the oil in the wok or frying-pan over medium heat and fry the onion for 7–8 minutes or until an even light brown, turning often, especially towards the end (a wok is helpful in frying the onions evenly, because if any pieces become too dark, you can push them up the side). Add the tomatoes with the flavourings and cook for 3–4 minutes more, pressing the lumps of tomato flesh against the bottom of the pan until dissolved. Add the meat and cook for 5–7 minutes, turning and pressing it against the base of the pan until thoroughly separated and mixed: make sure that no large lumps remain. Reduce the heat to low, add the carrots, potatoes and peas (if fresh and large) and simmer for 15 minutes. If the peas are fresh and small (that is, young), add when the other vegetables have been cooking for 10 minutes; if frozen, add when the vegetables have cooked for 13 minutes. Stir in the tomato purée and simmer very gently for about 7 minutes; if the sauce becomes very stiff, add just a little water.

3 Set brown rice to cook when you start frying the onions and white rice just after adding the meat to the pan. Rinse under the cold tap until the water runs clear, put into the saucepan with a lid, add 900 ml/1½ pints salted or unsalted water and bring to the boil. Stir, cover and simmer for 18 minutes for white Basmati, 20 minutes for other types of white rice or 30 minutes for brown. Leave to rest, covered, for 10 minutes and serve with the beef.

• STIR-FRIED BEEF WITH • SWEDE AND SPINACH

With the salty tang of oyster sauce, this very British set of ingredients makes an unexpectedly successful stir-fried dish. The beef is dear but you need relatively little and all the other items are cheap (at the time of going to press, the weight of rump steak needed costs about £1.50).

Use fresh, real spinach: sometimes, when proper spinach is unobtainable, a similar vegetable with larger leaves and thicker stems is sold instead. This is beet spinach, which is an acceptable substitute for some purposes but unsuitable here, since the leaves tend to disintegrate when stir-fried.

For 2–3

• INGREDIENTS •

250–375 g/8–12 oz Thai fragrant or white Patna or American long-grain rice

Salt

About 190 g/6 oz rump or minute steak, thinly cut

Pepper

4 teaspoons light soy sauce

3 tablespoons oil

1 teaspoon cornflour

Pinch of sugar

125 g/4 oz spinach

190 g/6 oz (2 medium to large) carrots

190 g/6 oz (½ small) swede

2 cloves garlic	3 tablespoons fresh or frozen chicken
1.5-cm/⅗-inch piece fresh root ginger	stock (see page 25) or 2 tablespoons water
3 teaspoons oyster sauce	

Saucepan with a lid (for the rice)
Wok or frying-pan

• METHOD •

1 Set the rice to simmer: rinse it under the cold tap until the water runs clear, put it into the saucepan with a lid and add 500 ml/ ⅔ pint salted or unsalted water for 250 g/8 oz rice or 750 ml/1¼ pints for 375 g/12 oz. Bring to the boil, stir, cover and simmer for 12 minutes for Thai rice or 20 minutes for other types of white rice. Leave to rest, covered, for 10–15 minutes.

2 Wash the steak in cold water, trim off and discard all the visible fat and cut across the grain into strips 2.5 cm/1 inch long and 5–6 mm/about ¼ inch wide (cutting across the grain promotes tenderness). Spread out on a plate and season moderately with pepper. Beat together 2 teaspoons of the soy sauce, 1 tablespoon of the oil, 1 tablespoon water, the cornflour and the sugar. Pour the mixture over the beef, toss thoroughly to mix and leave to infuse while you prepare the other ingredients.

3 Carefully pick over the spinach, removing any roots, weeds or damaged leaves. Wash, twice if necessary, cut into ribbons about 1 cm/½ inch wide and put into a sieve or colander or on a plate lined with kitchen paper to dry. Peel the carrots, cut into 2.5-cm/1-inch slices and cross-chop into sticks about 5mm/less than ¼ inch wide. Cut the swede in half; wrap the part you do not need in foodwrap and store in the refrigerator. Peel the part to be used, cut into 2.5-cm/1-inch slices and cross-chop into sticks of about the same size as the carrot. Peel and finely slice the garlic and ginger, removing any fibrous patches on the ginger. Mix the remaining 2 teaspoons soy sauce with the oyster sauce and stock or water.

4 Do not start stir-frying until the rice has simmered and rested. Check that the spinach is dry: blot with kitchen paper if necessary. Set all the prepared ingredients within easy reach of the cooker. Warm the remaining 2 tablespoons oil in the wok or frying-pan over high heat and add the garlic and ginger. Allow to fry for 30 seconds or until just starting to change colour. Add the carrot and stir; add the swede and stir-fry for 1½ minutes. Add the beef and stir-fry for 30 seconds or until just seared – that is, pale brown rather than red. Add the spinach and stir until it crumples. Pour in the sauce, stir for 20–30 seconds and serve with the rice.

· SALADS ·

Of the three styles of cooking included in this book, Thai is the only one in which salads play an important part, or at least salads made with raw vegetables. A Thai dinner might start with a carefully arranged selection of crudités, accompanied by a dipping sauce: the vegetables would then be left to refresh the tongue throughout the meal. In this chapter, I have given a few salads as meals, one of which is simply crudités, plus a hot (chilli-hot) sauce and rice. As well as this, however, I strongly recommend the Thai practice of serving raw vegetables as an accompaniment to hot, spicy dishes: you only need one or two, which can be selected purely on the basis of freshness and cost and will involve much less work than a conventional salad complete with dressing.

A point which deserves emphasis about rice salads in general is the excellence of soy or fish sauce combined with lemon juice as a dressing. With the addition of relatively little groundnut as opposed to olive oil (or even no oil at all if you prefer), the rice is so well flavoured that from the point of view of taste not much else is needed. In particular, this is exemplified by the chicken salad on page 138, where I have recommended crudités as extras rather than adding them to the salad itself because the chicken and rice are sufficient without them.

• RICE AND EGG •
SALAD WITH LEMON

This is an adaptation of another of Shehzad's recipes: the chief difference between this and the original is that I have substituted eggs for potatoes. It is delicately flavoured, refreshing and (at least to the European palate) unusual. Its only disadvantage is that the rice, eggs and peas all have to be boiled separately; however, squeezing a lemon, washing lettuce and chopping a little coriander are the only other preparations needed.

In summer, when they should have plenty of heart, ordinary round lettuces might be the best value. A crisper option with more flavour, however, is Cos, which are dearer but usually very much bigger, so that you will need only half. In winter, if you can afford it, use a couple of heads of chicory or Little Gem lettuces rather than a round, hothouse one, which will be neither crisp nor hearty.

Serve with Raita with Cucumber (page 28).

For 3–4

• INGREDIENTS •

375 g/12 oz brown or white Basmati (for preference), Patna or American long-grain rice

Salt

4 largish eggs

375 g/12 oz unpodded fresh or 125 g/4 oz frozen peas

1 smallish round, ½ large Cos or 2 Little Gem lettuces, or 2 heads chicory

Small bunch fresh coriander (enough for 1 tablespoon when chopped, plus 3–4 sprigs to decorate)

⅔ teaspoon black peppercorns

2 tablespoons olive oil

1 small or ½ large lemon

40 g/1½ oz sultanas

Saucepan with a lid (for the rice)

• METHOD •

1 Rinse the rice under the cold tap until the water runs clear. Put it into the saucepan with a lid, add 750 ml/1¼ pints salted or unsalted water and bring to the boil. Stir, cover and simmer for 18 minutes for white Basmati, 20 minutes for other types of white rice, or 30 minutes for all types of brown. Be especially careful to avoid overcooking. Leave to rest, covered, for 20–30 minutes; turn into a bowl and fluff up the grains with a fork.

2 Boil the eggs for 12 minutes and leave to cool. Pod the peas if necessary. Just cover with slightly salted water and boil for 5–15 minutes for fresh ones (how long they will take depends on their age) or 2 minutes for frozen. Drain and leave to cool.

3 Trim the root end of lettuce(s) or chicory, discard the outermost leaves and pull off the rest until you reach the hearts, removing any brown edges or patches. Divide the heart(s) into 2 or 4. Wash and leave to drain in a colander. Trim the ends of the coriander stems; wash the coriander, blot dry with kitchen paper and chop all but 3–4 sprigs fairly finely.

4 Crush the peppercorns and mix with 1 teaspoon salt and the oil. Squeeze the lemon and add 1 tablespoon plus 4 teaspoons of the juice to the mixture. Beat with a fork and pour over the rice. Separate the sultanas if necessary. Add with the peas and 1 tablespoon of the chopped coriander. Toss the rice thoroughly but gently.

5 Arrange the lettuce or chicory leaves around the edge of the salad bowl, keeping the hearts for the centre. Pile the dressed rice over them; make a well in the middle for the eggs. Shell and slice the eggs and arrange with the hearts in the well. Decorate with the reserved sprigs of coriander and serve.

• CRUDITÉS WITH TOFU AND • CHARRED CHILLI SAUCE

To take full advantage of the colours of the crudités, I suggest arranging them in bunches around a large, communal plate, with the other components of the meal in separate bowls. You can vary the selection of vegetables according to availability or which seem best value, but try to include at least two which are red, orange or yellow: for instance, you might replace the radishes below with a red or yellow pepper or (if you do not mind the price) cherry tomatoes.

It goes without saying that all the vegetables should be very fresh – that is, hard, firm and glossy. In my experience, organic produce generally (though not always) has more taste than that grown by the usual methods. Small, young carrots have better texture and tend to be sweeter than old ones; similarly, small radishes will probably be crisper than very large ones, which sometimes have fibrous holes in the middle.

A Thai cook might cut radish, carrot or cucumber-and-carrot flowers. Even if you do not favour fancy shapes, it makes an enormous difference to the appeal of the crudités if you cut them evenly and carefully.

The saucepan in which you fry the tofu should be fairly small to economize on oil but large enough to cover your ring completely, since hot oil is inflammable. The oil can be reused at least twice.

For 4

• INGREDIENTS •

310 g/10 oz Thai fragrant or brown or white Patna or American long-grain rice

Salt

About 280 g/9 oz tofu

About 600 ml/1 pint corn oil

4–5 cubes of stale bread (for testing the temperature of the oil)

500 g/1 lb (½ small) cauliflower

125 g/4 oz unsalted peanuts

2–3 inner sticks celery

190 g/6 oz (4 smallish) carrots

10-cm/4-inch length cucumber

1 green pepper

1 bunch radishes

½ lemon

2 tablespoons light soy sauce

½ quantity Vatch's Charred Chilli Sauce (see page 33)

Saucepan with a lid (for the rice)
Smallish, thick-based saucepan large enough to
cover your ring
Perforated spoon or fish-slice (if available)
Disposable cleaning-cloth (if available)
Small ovenproof dish
Sharp knife

• METHOD •

1 Rinse the rice under the cold tap until the water runs clear and put into the saucepan with a lid. Add 600 ml/1 pint water, salted if you wish, and bring to the boil. Stir, cover and simmer for 12 minutes for Thai rice, 20 minutes for other types of white rice, or 30 minutes for brown. Leave to stand, covered, for 20–30 minutes; loosen with a fork and turn into a bowl.

2 Rinse the tofu in cold water and squeeze in kitchen paper to remove surplus moisture. Chop into 1-cm/½-inch squares. Check that the smallish saucepan is perfectly dry. Pour corn oil into it to a depth of at least 3 cm/1¼ inches and set over high heat for 3 minutes: to minimize the risk of accidents, place it with the handle towards the back. Lower a cube of bread into the oil, taking care to avoid splashing: if it turns golden in the time it takes to count 20 – that is, in 20 seconds – the oil is hot enough for frying the tofu (it should be 190°C/375°F); remove the bread cube and discard. Reduce the heat to moderately low and place a plate lined with kitchen paper to hand near the cooker. Immerse a few of the pieces of tofu in the oil and fry for 1 minute or until they are pale gold and look rather like the squares of bread (if white). The pieces will tend to stick together as they fry: try to keep them separate. Remove with the perforated spoon or fish-slice (failing these, use a tablespoon). Place on the paper-lined plate to drain. Repeat until all the tofu is fried.

Leave the oil in the saucepan until cool. For reuse, strain through a sieve lined with a disposable cleaning-cloth, if available; otherwise, pour it slowly from the pan so that the impurities stay at the bottom; throw away the last couple of spoonfuls. Store in a covered jar or bottle.

3 Pre-heat the oven to 200°C/400°F/Gas Mark 6; put a saucepan of salted water on to boil. While the water heats,

halve the cauliflower; wrap the part you do not need in foodwrap and store in the refrigerator. Chop the half to be used into florets about 3 cm/1¼ inches across at the flower end and wash. When the water is boiling briskly, add the florets, bring the water back to the boil and cook for 3 minutes or until just (but only just) tender. Drain and immediately refresh under the cold tap (see page 16). Leave to cool. Spread the peanuts over the bottom of the ovenproof dish and bake in the oven for 10–12 minutes or until just showing signs of changing colour. Allow to cool.

4 Cut off the leaves and outside stalks from the celery and trim the root ends. Wash, dry and chop into 5-cm/2-inch lengths; then cross-chop into sticks 5 mm/less than ¼ inch wide. Scrub or peel the carrots and chop into sticks of the same size as the celery. Wash and dry the cucumber and chop into sticks of similar length but (because of its juiciness) a little wider. Wash, dry and quarter the pepper; throw away the core and seeds and trim off the white inner pith. Slice lengthways into strips about 5–6 mm/¼ inch wide. Wash and dry the radishes and cut off the roots and leaves, leaving short lengths of stem if you like.

5 Squeeze the lemon and mix 1 tablespoon of the juice with the soy sauce. Toss into the rice (which by now will be cool). Arrange the crudités on a dish; put the nuts and tofu into bowls. Serve with Charred Chilli Sauce (page 33).

• BEANSPROUT SALAD WITH • CELERY AND PEANUTS

With carrots and red pepper, bright-green beans and pale-green celery, this is a particularly attractive-looking salad; it is also very healthy, very satisfying and fairly cheap.

The pepper should be hard and glossy, the beans firm and crisp and the beansprouts as fresh as possible (look at the sell-by date). Small carrots have a better texture and will probably be sweeter than large ones: best of all, choose organic.

It is up to you whether or not to skin the pepper, as directed. It is a nuisance and not essential, especially as it is cut into small dice, but some people (including myself) find the skin irritatingly tough; skinning also adds to the flavour of the salad by contributing a slightly charred taste and helping to release the sweet juices.

For 4

• INGREDIENTS •

280–310 g/9–10 oz Thai fragrant or white Patna or American long-grain rice

Salt

190 g/6 oz mixed beansprouts

90 g/3 oz Kenya or other fine, stringless, green beans

2-cm/¾-inch piece fresh root ginger

125 g/4 oz unsalted peanuts

1 red pepper

3 inner sticks celery

150 g/5 oz (3 or 4 smallish) carrots

1 moderately hot green chilli

½ small lemon

1 teaspoon sugar

1 tablespoon light soy sauce

1 tablespoon dark soy sauce

1 tablespoon oil, plus a little more if you plan to skin the pepper and your rings are electric

Saucepan with a lid (for the rice)
1 or 2 small baking-trays (2 will save a little time if you wish to skin the pepper and your rings are electric)
Tongs or oven-glove (if you wish to skin the pepper and your rings are gas)
Foodbag or foodwrap (for skinning the pepper)

• METHOD •

1 Place the rice in a sieve and rinse under the cold tap until the water runs clear; put into the saucepan with a lid. Add 560 ml/19 fl oz water, salted or otherwise, for 280 g/9 oz or 600ml/ 1 pint for 310 g/10 oz rice. Bring to the boil, stir, cover and simmer gently for 12 minutes for Thai rice or 20 minutes for other types of white rice. Leave to stand, covered, for 20–30 minutes; loosen with a fork and transfer to a bowl or serving dish.

2 Thoroughly pick over and wash the beansprouts. Top and tail the beans, wash and chop into 2-cm/¾-inch lengths. Peel and finely slice the ginger, discarding any fibrous patches. Bring a second saucepan of water to a vigorous boil, add a pinch of salt, the ginger, beans and beansprouts, bring back to a brisk boil and cook for 3 minutes (but no longer). Drain through a sieve and refresh under the cold tap (see page 16). Leave in the sieve to dry.

3 Pre-heat the oven to 220°C/425°F/Gas Mark 7. Spread out the nuts on a baking-tray and roast for 5–6 minutes or until just showing signs of changing colour.

4 For skinning the pepper, see Tomato Chutney with Red Pepper on page 31. Having peeled it, wipe away any charred remains of skin from the flesh, place in a bowl and cut into quarters; reserve the juice which will emerge. Discard the core, seeds and inner pith and dice the flesh into pea-sized squares. Put into a salad bowl.

5 Trim the leaves and root ends of the celery; wash, dry and pare off any discoloured streaks. Cut into 2-cm/¾-inch slices and cross-chop into sticks 5 mm/less than ¼ inch wide. Add to the salad bowl. Scrub or peel the carrots; slice and chop into sticks of the same size and add. Wash and dry the chilli; trim the stalk end, remove the inner membrane and seeds and finely dice the flesh; add to the salad bowl. Do not touch your eyes while chopping it and wash your hands afterwards.

6 Add the beans, beansprouts and nuts to the salad bowl. Squeeze the lemon and beat 2 teaspoons of the juice with the sugar, the juice from the pepper, the soy sauces and 1 tablespoon oil. Pour over the salad and toss. Serve the rice separately.

• LEFT-OVER CHICKEN •
AND RICE SALAD

You may feel that I am cheating in calling this a recipe at all because it is so simple and easy – which, however, seems to me all the more reason to include it. The point of it is to use up the chicken meat left over from making stock (see page 25). Apart from the chicken, all you need is rice, lettuce, a chilli and half a lemon (plus soy sauce). I have tried adding further ingredients but it is so good as it is that every other item seemed detrimental. A better idea than putting them into the salad itself is to serve crudités such as green pepper and/or radishes separately.

Use a large Cos lettuce when available, as its sweetness especially suits the salad. The next best alternative is a Little Gem, which is similar but dearer and very small. Ordinary round lettuces are much cheaper and in summer, when they should be fat and hearty, often very good value; in winter, however, when they are hothouse grown, they are usually thin and tasteless.

Use the chicken as soon as possible after taking if from the stock saucepan so that it does not become dry. If you are obliged to keep it until the next day, do not chop it up but toss it in a teaspoonful of the soy sauce and store (covered) in the refrigerator.

For 3

• INGREDIENTS •

310 g/10 oz Thai fragrant or white Patna or American long-grain rice

Salt

½ large or 1 small Cos lettuce or 2 Little Gem or 1 round lettuce

1 bunch radishes (optional)

1 green pepper (optional)

1 mild green chilli

½ lemon

2 tablespoons soy sauce

Pepper

Meat from 2 chicken legs

Saucepan with a lid (for the rice)

• METHOD •

1 Rinse the rice under the cold tap until the water runs clear and put into the saucepan with a lid. Add 600 ml/1 pint water, with a little salt if you wish, and bring to the boil. Stir, cover and simmer for 12 minutes for Thai rice or 20 minutes for other

types of white rice. Leave to stand, covered, for 20–30 minutes; loosen with a fork and allow to become cold.

2 Discard the outermost layer of the lettuce, trim the root end and separate into leaves. Wash in cold water and put into a colander to drain. If you do not need all of it, put the spare leaves into an airtight bag and store in the refrigerator. Cut the roots and leaves from the radishes; if you like, leave about 5–6 mm/¼ inch of stalk. Wash in cold water and leave to drain. Wash, dry and quarter the pepper; discard the core, seeds and pale inner pith and cut the flesh into strips about 5–6 mm/¼ inch wide. Wash and dry the chilli and trim the stalk end; remove the inner membrane and seeds and dice the flesh as finely as possible. Taste one of the pieces: if it is hot rather than mild, do not use all of it. Avoid rubbing your eyes while handling it and wash your hands directly afterwards.

3 Squeeze the lemon. Mix 4 teaspoons of the juice with the soy sauce and add a moderate seasoning of pepper. Toss into the rice. Chop the chicken fairly small; toss into the rice with the chilli. Line a salad bowl with the lettuce and pile the dressed chicken and rice in the middle. Serve the radishes and green pepper separately.

• SWEET RICE DISHES •

This chapter really should not be here at all, since the students who laid down the blue-print for the books said that they never made puddings except when they were giving parties. However, rice puddings are so easy and cheap to make that it seemed a pity not to include a few, especially as sweet puddings and pullaos are traditional in India. I have cheated in giving a British slant to the first group of recipes, which are made by my own method and with the option of Western pudding rice; also, one of the recipes is purely my own, with no pretensions to being Oriental apart from being flavoured with coconut milk. However, the last is a rich, aromatic, Indian pudding made with ground, rather than pudding, rice and nothing like the traditional British version.

• SWEET SPICED OR • FLAVOURED RICE

I have deliberately not called this series of recipes rice puddings (although they are) in the hope that those who claim to hate them might at least read this far. Yes, they are rice puddings – but interestingly flavoured with spices or coconut, and light, creamy or sticky according to the rice you choose. Not only are they cheap and easy to make, but even fairly healthy, since they contain milk but no added fat and need relatively little sweetening. They can be simmered or baked, eaten hot or cold and served alone, with fruit or with cream.

The traditional British rice pudding is made with short grained, so-called 'pudding' rice, which releases starch as it cooks to produce a thick, creamy sauce; the grains, however, do not entirely break down but retain a nutty centre. In the East, sweet dishes are sometimes made with glutinous or 'sticky' rice, which breaks down almost entirely into a gluey paste. You can also make puddings with Thai fragrant rice, which becomes very soft when cooked for a long time but releases less starch and gives a lighter result.

Glutinous rice can be bought only from Oriental stores; it is not essential for any of the following recipes, but you may like to try it. It has a distinctive taste: hot, its stickiness is something like tapioca; cold, it resembles blancmange.

For eating cold, puddings should be simmered rather than baked: simmering is also quicker and saves fuel. To addicts, however, part of the joy of rice puddings is the skin which forms on baked ones (assuming that you bake them in milk rather than coconut milk, which will not produce skin); baking also produces a slightly different, more concentrated flavour. I have suggested raw fruit to go with cold puddings but, although plain hot ones go excellently with stewed fruit, I recommend eating the flavoured versions given here alone.

• SIMMERED SWEET •
SPICED RICE

Allow 1–2 hours for soaking the rice before simmering (this is not essential for pudding rice); the cooking time is 1¼–1½ hours, or 1 hour for glutinous rice.

Serve hot, warm or cold, alone if hot or with mango, pears or Asian pears and/or whipped cream on top if cold.

Asian pears can be bought from some supermarkets or at Oriental stores. They look rather like ripe Golden Delicious apples and have a delicate flavour which goes well with spices.

For 2–3 alone, or 3–4 with additions

• INGREDIENTS •

50 g/2 oz pudding, Thai fragrant or glutinous rice

2 cardamom pods

2 cloves

2.5-cm/1-inch stick cinnamon

90g/3oz sugar

750–900 ml/1¼–1½ pints milk for Thai fragrant or pudding rice, or 600 ml/1 pint for glutinous rice

1 scant teaspoon garam masala (see page 21)

150 ml/¼ pint double cream (optional)

2 or 3 pears, 2 Asian pears or 1 mango (optional)

• METHOD •

1 Rinse the rice and cover with cold water; leave for 1–2 hours (if you are using pudding rice, soaking is not essential). Rinse again. Bruise the cardamoms in a mortar so that the pods are open (leave the cloves and cinnamon whole). Put the rice, sugar and spices into a saucepan with 600 ml/1 pint milk and bring to the boil. Stir, lower the heat and simmer gently, uncovered, for 1 hour; stir at intervals and frequently for the last 10 minutes. Glutinous rice will now be ready; with pudding or Thai fragrant rice, add another 150 ml/¼ pint milk, stir and simmer for a further 15 minutes, stirring constantly for the last 5 minutes. For an extra-creamy pudding, add another 150 ml/ ¼ pint milk and simmer for 15 minutes more, again stirring constantly towards the end. Sprinkle with the garam masala and either serve hot or allow to cool.

2 To serve cold, whip the cream (if using) until stiff and spread over the top, or prepare the fruit. Quarter, core, peel and slice pears or Asian pears: as they tend to turn brown on exposure to air, sprinkle with just a little sugar and a few drops of lemon juice. For how to prepare a mango, see page 165.

• BAKED SWEET •
SPICED RICE

Allow 1–2 hours for soaking Thai fragrant or glutinous rice plus 1¾–2 hours respectively for baking, or 3 hours for baking pudding rice.

With Thai rice, I suggest making a stiffer pudding with less milk.

For 3

• INGREDIENTS •

50 g/2 oz glutinous, Thai fragrant
or pudding rice

2 cardamom pods

2 cloves

2.5-cm/1-inch stick cinnamon

90 g/3 oz sugar

1 scant teaspoon garam masala

900 ml/1½ pints milk for pudding
rice, 750 ml/1¼ pints for glutinous
rice, or 600 ml/1 pint for Thai rice

Ovenproof dish about 16 cm/6¼ inches across and
9cm/3½ inches deep

• METHOD •

Rinse Thai fragrant or glutinous rice in a sieve under the cold tap until the water runs clear, and leave to soak in cold water for 1–2 hours; rinse again. Rinse pudding rice in the same way. Pre-heat the oven to 120°C/250°F/Gas Mark ½. Bruise the cardamoms in a mortar so that the pods are open; leave all the other spices whole. Put all the ingredients except the garam masala into the ovenproof dish, stir thoroughly and bake for 45 minutes. Remove from the oven, stir again and bake for another 30 minutes. With Thai and glutinous rice, stir in the garam masala and bake for a further 30 or 45 minutes respectively. With pudding rice, stir and bake for another 45 minutes; stir in the garam masala and bake for a further hour. Serve hot.

• FOUR-SPICE RICE PUDDING •

This is a version of Chinese five-spice pudding: I have left out the fifth spice, Sichuan peppercorns, because they can be bought only at Oriental stores. Prepared five-spice powder is sometimes sold at health-food and other shops; however, since it will not be freshly ground, it will have a shallower, less distinctive taste than the four freshly crushed or whole spices given below. Also, because of its fineness, it is difficult to mix into the pudding: it tends to float on top. Star anise, which has a liquorice flavour, can be bought at some supermarkets or good grocers or health-food shops.

As in the previous recipes, the pudding may be simmered or baked. Serve alone if hot, or with whipped cream and/or pears or Asian pears if cold.

Allow 1-2 hours for soaking the rice.

For 2–4

• INGREDIENTS •

50 g/2 oz pudding, Thai fragrant or glutinous rice

⅛ teaspoon fennel seeds

½ star anise

4 cloves

1.5-cm/⅔-inch stick cinnamon

90 g/3 oz sugar

600 ml/1 pint milk for simmered glutinous or baked Thai rice, 750 ml/1¼ pints for baked glutinous rice, 750–900 ml/1¼–1½ pints for simmered Thai or pudding rice, or 900 ml/1½ pints for baked pudding rice

Ovenproof dish about 16 cm/6¼ inches across and 9 cm/3½ inches deep (if baking)

• METHOD •

Rinse the rice and soak in cold water for 1–2 hours (soaking is not essential for pudding rice). Rinse again. Crush the fennel seeds, star anise and cloves to a powder in a mortar; leave the cinnamon whole. For a simmered pudding, put the rice, spices and sugar into a saucepan with 600 ml/1 pint milk and proceed as for Simmered Sweet Spiced Rice (page 142). For a baked pudding, put all the ingredients into the ovenproof dish and continue as for Baked Sweet Spiced Rice (page 144).

• COCONUT RICE •

For this you can use milk made from fresh or desiccated coconut (see page 24) or tinned coconut milk. If sweet, fresh coconut will give the best flavour. Tinned coconut milk is relatively thick and thus gives a good texture: I particularly recommend it with Thai rice. Some tinned milk, however, is grey and will make a greyish or brownish pudding, which will be the greyer or browner if spices are added.

As one nut, tin or packet of desiccated coconut yields only 450 ml/¾ pint milk, make up the quantity with ordinary milk. Remember that coconut milk is not nutritious in the same way as cow's milk.

Either of the spiced puddings above can be made with coconut, but in general I prefer them with cow's milk; one exception, however, is hot Baked Sweet Spiced Rice made with glutinous rice, which is brilliant with coconut milk (but it must be eaten hot: it is disgusting cold).

Serve this dish cold with mango, pears or Asian pears as before, or (very un-Oriental but excellent) raspberries; or serve hot on its own or with raspberry conserve or jam.

Allow 1–2 hours for Thai or glutinous rice to soak.

For 2–4

• INGREDIENTS •

50 g/2 oz pudding, Thai fragrant or glutinous rice

90 g/3 oz sugar

450 ml/¾ pint coconut milk

150 ml/¼ pint milk for simmered glutinous or baked Thai rice, 300 ml/ ½ pint for baked glutinous rice, 300–450 ml/½–¾ pint for simmered Thai or pudding rice, or 450 ml/¾ pint for baked pudding rice

Ovenproof dish about 16cm/6¼ inches across and 9cm/3½ inches deep (if baking)

• METHOD •

Rinse the rice and soak for 1–2 hours; rinse again. Put it into a saucepan or the ovenproof dish with the sugar, coconut milk and milk as for Simmered or Baked Sweet Spiced Rice; continue as on pages 142–144.

• COCONUT RICE DOUGHNUTS •

These have no claim to being Oriental: I invented them partly as a joke and called them doughnuts because they are fried, rolled in sugar and have jam in the middle. However, as they do not contain dough, I suppose that really I should have named them 'rice-nuts'.

As the rice cannot be moulded until it is cold, it must be simmered in advance: I suggest cooking it the previous day (store, covered, in the refrigerator). Allow 1–2 hours for it to soak before simmering.

The saucepan used for frying should be smallish to economize on oil but must be large enough to cover your ring.

Makes 8–12 nuts, according to size

• INGREDIENTS •

150 g/5 oz Thai fragrant or American long-grain rice

150 g/5 oz sugar

450 ml/¾ pint coconut milk (see page 24)

300 ml/½ pint milk

4–6 teaspoons raspberry conserve or jam

600 ml/1 pint or more corn oil

4–5 small cubes of stale bread (for testing the temperature of the oil)

Smallish, thick-based saucepan large enough to cover your ring
Perforated spoon (if available)

• METHOD •

1 Rinse the rice, soak for 1–2 hours and rinse again. Put into a saucepan (any) with 90 g/3 oz of the sugar, the coconut milk and 150 ml/¼ pint of ordinary milk. Bring to the boil, stir and simmer, uncovered, for 45 minutes; stir from time to time and constantly for the last 5 minutes. Add the remaining 150 ml/¼ pint milk, bring back to a simmer and cook for a further 15 minutes, again stirring constantly for the last 5 minutes. Remove from the heat, allow to cool and chill in the refrigerator.

2 Mould about a dessertspoon of the rice into a thickish disc in the palm of your hand and indent the middle using your finger. Put ½ teaspoon of jam into the indentation (do not add more or you will have great difficulty in preventing it from escaping). Place a lump of rice over the jam and form into a solid ball, sealing any jammy cracks round the sides with smaller lumps of rice. Repeat until all the rice is moulded. The exact size of the balls is not important, but they should be smaller than the usual doughnut (say, about the size of a tangerine).

3 Check that the smallish saucepan is perfectly dry. Pour oil into it to a depth of 3.5 cm/1⅓ inches or more: there should be enough to cover the balls by at least 2 cm/¾ inch. Set over high heat for 3 minutes; as a safety precaution, turn the handle towards the back. While the oil heats, sprinkle the remaining 50 g/2 oz sugar evenly over a plate and line two more plates with kitchen paper: set all three plates within easy reach of the cooker. Test the temperature of the oil by lowering one of the squares of bread into it: be careful to avoid splashing. If it turns golden in the time it takes to count 20 – that is, in 20 seconds – the oil is hot enough to start frying (it should be 190°C/375°F). Remove the cube of bread and discard. Reduce the heat to medium/low. Carefully lower in one or two of the balls and allow to fry for 1¾–2 minutes or until a rich brown: do not disturb them as they fry until they are well browned or the crust will break and some of the rice will stick to the spoon. If this happens, wash and dry the spoon or use another, as the rice on the spoon will in turn stick to the balls. Lift out the balls with a perforated spoon (if available); otherwise, use a tablespoon (rather than a fish-slice, since the corners of a slice may pierce the rice crust). Place on one of the plates lined with kitchen paper. Lower the next balls into the oil and repeat until all are fried. Then re-fry each just for a few seconds: this will give a crisper crust. Place on the second plate lined with kitchen paper. Finally roll in the sugar and allow to cool (you can eat them while still warm, but they taste better cold).

• GROUND RICE PUDDING • WITH NUTS AND CARDAMOM

Like Tomatoes Stuffed with Mint and Walnuts, this recipe is adapted from *Anpurna Part* 4 (Shree Oshwal Mahila Mandal). I remember that when I first tried it, I stared at the lumpy brownish mass heaving in the saucepan and thought grimly: 'It had better taste good.' It did: I could not stop eating it all evening. On that occasion I made it a little too stiff and (because I did not have any) omitted the saffron, which transforms the brown into a deep corn yellow. However, saffron is expensive: as it is not essential to taste, I leave it as optional (in this one instance, I suggest using it in powdered form, which is cheaper).

The pudding should be served very hot, either alone, with a few grapes, or Indian-style at the same time as a curry.
For 6–8

• INGREDIENTS •

50 g/2 oz unskinned almonds or peanuts

50 g/2 oz shelled pistachio nuts

8 cardamom pods

50 g/2 oz cashew nuts

900 ml/1½ pints milk

250 g/8 oz sugar

1 sachet saffron powder (optional)

50 g/2 oz butter

45 g/scant 2 oz ground rice

50 g/2 oz desiccated coconut

Small baking tray (for crisping the nuts; optional)

• METHOD •

1 It is desirable to crisp the almonds and pistachio nuts in the oven, but expensive unless you are using the oven anyway. If you are, spread the nuts on the baking tray and bake for 8–10 minutes at 200°C/400°F/Gas Mark 6. Allow to cool a little. Crush roughly in a mortar, leaving some larger pieces. Bruise the cardamoms to release the seeds; discard the pods and leave the seeds in the mortar. Add the cashew nuts to the mortar and crush to a paste.

2 Heat but do not boil the milk. Remove from the heat, add the sugar and stir in the saffron (if using). Using another saucepan, melt the butter over moderate/low heat and add the ground rice. Fry, stirring constantly, for 3 minutes or until the rice has turned pale brown. Remove from the heat and stir in the coconut and cashew nuts with the cardamom seeds. Add the milk, almonds and pistachios, reduce the heat to very low and cook for 10–15 minutes or until the mixture is thick but still liquid. Serve at once.

• DINNER-PARTIES •

When you have friends to dinner, you may want to serve more than one dish (apart from rice). The Eastern custom is to serve extra dishes, rather than more of the same dish, according to the number of diners. I do not suggest going too far in this direction, but if you plan carefully you can cook two or three items together without difficulty. These items should be of contrasting textures and flavours: it is also desirable that only one should demand last-minute attention. For both these reasons, they should not include more than one stir-fried dish, although you might add a deep-fried item which can be re-fried quickly when stir-frying is finished. To make cooking easier, it is a good idea to choose at least one dish that can be prepared in advance. There are a number of menus you can compose on this basis: the following are only examples.

For a vegetarian Indian-style dinner for 4–6, you could serve Shobhna's Paneer and Tomato Sauce (page 64), Chick-pea and Potato Cakes (page 177) and Spinach Rice (page 40). Potato cakes can be prepared in advance and fried at the last minute (you will have to fry, rather than bake, them because the rice calls for a lower oven heat). For a non-vegetarian dinner, I suggest Shehzad's Tandoori-style Chicken (page 106), Raita with Cucumber and Mint (page 29), plus Braised Broccoli with Lemon and Coriander (page 163) and plain rice.

For a vegetarian Chinese-style dinner for 3–4, I recommend Sweet-and-sour Aubergine with Peanuts and Beansprouts (page 91), Steamed Eggs (page 80) and plain rice: do not start frying the aubergine until the Steamed Eggs are cooked. For non-vegetarians, an easy and festive option is the Red-baked Beef with Tofu and Mushrooms or Red-cooked Chicken with Shiitake Mushrooms, plus Pork with Oyster Sauce and Kohlrabi and plain rice: these should be enough for 4–6. For a Thai-style meal for 3–4, serve Seafood Curry with Lime Zest or Lemon Grass and Deep-Fried Tofu Balls, either plain or with ginger (page 68) and plain rice. Fry the tofu balls before cooking the curry but keep the oil hot and re-fry briefly when the curry is ready. Alternatively, fry and serve the balls as a snack before the meal.

If you want a dessert, I suggest fruit, fruit salad or ices (sweet rice dishes are unsuitable because the main courses are already served with rice). Fruit tends to be expensive, but you can sometimes buy smallish pineapples for under £1. As with coconuts, they sometimes lack sweetness but if you choose one that is golden all over rather than green at the base, there is a fair chance that it will be delicious. It should give slightly to the touch, but not much. To prepare it, cut off the top and bottom and peel the skin away with a sharp knife, either peeling thickly enough to remove the eyes under the skin or trimming them off in Vs. Slice fairly thickly and cut out the hard core as tidily as you can. Other fruit possibilities are sliced oranges or a bunch of grapes. Choose small, navel or blood oranges, allowing 6–8 for 4–6 people. Prepare as for the orange in the fruit salad on page 164; sprinkle with 50 g/2 oz sugar and (except blood oranges) the juice of 1 lime or ½ a lemon, and chill for 2–3 hours. Grapes should be glossy and firmly attached to their stems; if they are dropping off, they are overripe. White seem to me more suitable after a Chinese-style meal than black; best of all are seedless, which are usually very sweet. To prepare, wash thoroughly under the cold tap and leave in a colander to drain.

• RED-BAKED BEEF •
WITH TOFU AND MUSHROOMS

As it is easy to make and benefits from being prepared and partly cooked in advance, this is an ideal dish for dinner-parties, although I would not limit serving it to special occasions only. When you are entertaining, use high-quality beef: the first time I tried it, I used Aberdeen Angus and it was sensational; however, it is also an exceptionally good way of cooking relatively cheap, anonymous stewing-steak (at the time of going to press this cost approximately £1.70 per 500 g/1 lb).

I have added tofu not merely because it makes the meat go further but because it absorbs the flavour of the sauce and, in my opinion, ends up even better than the beef.

The total cooking time for the dish is 4¼–5 hours. However, I recommend cooking it for 2½ hours the day before you plan to eat it: this gives the rich flavour time to develop and offers a good opportunity to skim off any beef fat, which will solidify on top of the sauce when it has cooled.

For a party, serve this with Stir-fried Pork with Oyster Sauce and Kohlrabi (see page 158).

For 4–5

• INGREDIENTS •

500 g/1 lb stewing-beef

Pepper

150 g/5 oz tofu

190 g/6 oz button mushrooms

3 cloves garlic

2.5-3-cm/1-1¼-inch piece fresh root ginger

2 tablespoons oil

450 ml/¾ pint fresh or frozen chicken stock (see page 25)

5 tablespoons light soy sauce

3 tablespoons medium-dry sherry

1 level teaspoon soft dark-brown sugar

375–500 g/12 oz–1 lb Thai fragrant or white Patna or American long-grain rice

Wok or frying-pan
Casserole 18–20 cm/7–8 inches across and 6–7.5 cm/2½–3
inches deep
Saucepan with lid (for the rice)

• METHOD •

1 Trim all the visible fat from the beef and cut into 2-cm/¾-inch cubes. Wash in cold water and leave to soak in fresh, cold water for 15–20 minutes. Set on a plate lined with kitchen paper to dry and season fairly generously with pepper.
2 Slice as much tofu as you need from the block: to keep the rest, either follow the instructions on the packet or immerse in cold water, cover and store for up to 3 days in the refrigerator. Rinse the part to be used under the cold tap and squeeze in kitchen paper to remove surplus moisture. Cut into triangles with sides of about 1 cm/½ inch. Trim the mushroom stalks; wash and finely slice the mushrooms and season moderately with pepper. Peel and finely slice the garlic and ginger, removing any fibrous patches on the ginger.
3 Check that the beef is dry. Warm the oil over high heat in the wok or frying-pan, add the garlic and ginger and allow to fry until just starting to change colour. Add the beef and stir-fry until seared (that is, pale brown rather than red but not dark brown) on all sides. Remove from the heat.
4 Pre-heat the oven to 150°C/300°F/Gas Mark 2. Arrange half the beef in a layer at the bottom of the casserole. Add the tofu and mushrooms and spread the rest of the meat, with the garlic, ginger and cooking juice, on top. Mix together the stock, soy sauce, sherry and sugar and pour over the meat. Cover and bake in the oven for 4¼–4¾ hours if you are serving it on the same day or 2½ hours on the first day and 2–2½ hours on the second (the extra 15 minutes is to allow for the dish to reheat). Store overnight either in the refrigerator or in a cool place (leave it in the casserole). Before returning it to the oven on the second day, remove any solid fat from the top. When ready, the meat should be very tender but not quite falling apart, and just, or almost, covered with sauce: look at it after it has cooked for 3¼–3½ hours and, if the sauce is much reduced, turn down the oven to 120°C/250°F/Gas Mark ½.
5 Start simmering the rice when the meat has been in the

oven for about 4 hours if you are cooking it in one day or for 1¼ hours on the second day (exact timing is not important: the meat will come to no harm if cooked for an extra 10–20 minutes, and the rice will stay hot on top of the warm oven for up to 30 minutes. Rinse the rice until the water runs clear, put into the saucepan with a lid and add 750 ml/1¼ pints water for 375 g/12 oz rice or 980 ml/1⅔ pints for 500 g/1 lb. Bring to the boil, stir, cover and simmer for 12 minutes for Thai rice or 20 minutes for other types of rice; leave to rest, covered, for at least 10 minutes before serving with the beef.

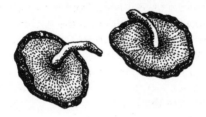

• RED-BAKED CHICKEN •
WITH SHIITAKE MUSHROOMS

Like red-baked beef, this is particularly suitable for a dinner-party because it involves relatively little work and needs no last-minute attention. As with the beef, it is a good idea to start preparing it the day before, since the stock takes 3–4 hours to simmer. Assuming that you use a whole bird (which is more economical anyway), a chicken will supply not only its own stock but also a generous surplus which you can freeze too (see page 25). A butcher will cut up the chicken for you, but provided that you have a sharp knife you will find it surprisingly easy to do it yourself. Alternatively, you can use ready-cut portions; however this will mean making the stock separately.

If the chicken is cut up by a butcher, remember that you want the carcase as well as the meat.

The shiitake mushrooms are a luxury but have a unique pronounced flavour. If you buy in large quantities, they will be considerably cheaper £ for lb (or rather, £ for g/oz). However, at the time of going to press a small (that is, 50-g/2-oz packet) will set you back at least £1.75. You will need half (25 g/1 oz) for this recipe: use the rest for congee (see page 54). You are unlikely to be able to buy shiitake mushrooms in all supermarkets but they will be stocked at any Oriental store. Serve with plain rice, Stir-Fried Pork with Oyster Sauce and Kohlrabi (page 158) and, if you want a fourth dish, Deep-fried Tofu Balls with Ginger, or Tofu and Prawn Balls (pages 68–70).

For 4

• INGREDIENTS •

1 smallish chicken or 4 chicken quarters

4 black peppercorns

25 g/1 oz (9 or 10) dried shiitake mushrooms

190 g/6 oz button mushrooms

3 cloves garlic

2-cm/¾-inch piece fresh root ginger

Pepper

1 level teaspoon sugar

4 tablespoons light soy sauce

310–375 g/10–12 oz Thai fragrant or white Patna or American long-grain rice

Sharp knife for cutting up the chicken
Large saucepan with a lid
Casserole about 20 cm/8 inches across and
7.5 cm/3 inches deep
Saucepan with a lid (for the rice)

• METHOD •

1 Thoroughly wash the chicken inside and out with cold water. If it has been cut up by a butcher, wash the carcase as well as the portions. If not, put it on a board or other chopping surface or, if you have nowhere else, in the sink. Turn it breast downwards and cut around the legs, as close to the ribs as possible, using the sharp knife: the joint at the top can be separated with a sharp twist. Turn the bird over and cut off the breast portions by slicing along each side of the breast-bone as far as the wings: leave the wings on the carcase. Unless you feel strongly about fat, try to keep the skin, which adds richness to the dish, on all the portions. However, as it is tougher than the meat, you may find that the skin pulls off the breasts, in which case leave them skinned and place them underneath the legs in the casserole.

2 Set the chicken portions on a plate and cover with foodwrap or another plate; if you are preparing the chicken in advance, store in the refrigerator. Remove any skin from the carcase and put the carcase into the large saucepan with a lid. Wash your hands, and also the knife and chopping-surface. Add the peppercorns to the saucepan, plus 1.5 litres/2½ pints water, or just enough to cover the carcase. Bring to the boil and skim. Put on the lid and simmer for 3–4 hours; strain, throw away the bones and fragments of meat (which are not worth saving) and allow to cool. Pour off and reserve 300 ml/½ pint stock for the chicken; reduce and freeze the rest (see pages 24–25). If you are preparing the chicken ahead of time, cover the 300ml/½ pint and store either in the refrigerator or somewhere cool.

3 Pour 300 ml/½ pint hot (but not boiling) water over the shiitake mushrooms and leave to soften for 25 minutes. Finely slice the caps; if possible, use the stalks for vegetable stock, but otherwise discard them. Reserve the soaking liquor (as the mushrooms will have absorbed most of it, only a little will be left). Trim the stalks of the button mushrooms; wash, dry and slice finely. Peel and finely slice the garlic and ginger, rejecting any fibrous patches on the ginger.

4 Pre-heat the oven to 200°C/400°F/Gas Mark 6. Place both sorts of mushroom in the bottom of the casserole. Season moderately with pepper and sprinkle with some of the garlic and ginger. Put the chicken on top; if the breasts are skinned, arrange them as far as possible under the legs, but otherwise set the pieces so that they are evenly exposed. Season with pepper again and sprinkle with the rest of the garlic and ginger. Make up the mushroom liquor to 300 ml/½ pint with stock; add the sugar and soy sauce, pour into the casserole and bake for 1 hour 10 minutes. Take off the lid and bake for a further 10–20 minutes, until the chicken is lightly browned, very tender, and exudes no pink liquid when pierced with a knife or skewer in the thickest part. If the sauce is much reduced, add the remaining chicken stock.

5 Set the rice to simmer when the chicken has been cooking for about an hour. Rinse under the cold tap until the water runs clear and put into the saucepan with a lid. Add 600 ml/1 pint water for 310 g/10 oz rice or 750 ml/1¼ pints for 375 g/12 oz (because of the saltiness of the soy sauce, you will not need to add salt). Bring to the boil and stir. Cover and simmer for 12 minutes for Thai rice or 20 minutes for other types of rice; leave to stand, covered, for 10–20 minutes. Serve with the chicken.

• STIR-FRIED PORK WITH •
OYSTER SAUCE AND
KOHLRABI

I have included this here because it goes especially well with red-cooked beef or chicken: in contrast to the richness of the red-baked dishes, it is crisp, light and refreshing. However, you can also serve it as a main course on its own, accompanied by plain rice and Red-Chilli Oil. The quantities of rice given below are for serving alone.

If you cannot find kohlrabi, use swede instead.

For 4

• INGREDIENTS •

1 egg (white only)

125–190 g/4–6 oz thin-cut pork chops

Salt

2 tablespoons oil

1 teaspoon cornflour

375–450 g/12–14 oz Thai fragrant or white Patna or American long-grain rice

150 g/5 oz mung beansprouts

190 g/6 oz (3 medium) carrots

225 g/7 oz (½ medium or 1 small) kohlrabi or 1 medium swede

2 cloves garlic

1-cm/½-inch piece fresh root ginger

2 teaspoons light soy sauce

2 teaspoons oyster sauce

4 tablespoons vegetable stock or water

Saucepan with a lid (for the rice)
Wok or frying-pan
Perforated spoon (if available)

• METHOD •

1 Separate the egg: wash and dry the shell and crack it sharply in the middle of the edge of a small bowl. Hold it over the bowl and tip the yolk from one half of the shell to the other until all the white has fallen out. You will not need the yolk for this recipe, so if possible add it to an omelette or scrambled eggs. Store it in a cup, covered, in the refrigerator and use within 24 hours.

2 Wash the pork and dry with kitchen paper. Trim off all the fat and cut into strips 2 cm/¾ inch long and 5–6 mm/¼ inch wide. Season very lightly with salt and toss in ½ tablespoon (3 teaspoons) of the oil. Sprinkle with the cornflour and toss again. Add the egg white and toss for a third time. Leave while you prepare the rest of the ingredients.

3 Rinse the rice until the water runs clear and put into the saucepan with a lid. Add 750 ml/1¼ pints water for 375 g/12 oz or 900 ml/1½ pints for 450 g/14 oz rice; add a pinch of salt, if desired. Bring to the boil, stir, cover and simmer for 10–12 minutes for Thai rice or 20 minutes for Patna or American long-grain rice. Leave to stand, covered, for 10 minutes.

4 Pick over and thoroughly rinse the beansprouts; leave in a sieve or colander to drain. Peel the carrots and chop into strips 2 cm/¾ inch long and 5 mm/less than ¼ inch wide. Halve the kohlrabi or swede, if necessary. Wrap the half you do not need in foodwrap and store in the refrigerator; peel and chop the half to be used into strips of the same size as the carrot. Peel and finely slice the garlic and ginger, removing any tough, fibrous patches on the ginger; keep the two cloves of garlic separate.

5 Set all the prepared ingredients plus a clean plate and the soy and oyster sauce to hand near the cooker. Blot the beansprouts with kitchen paper, Warm 1½ tablespoons of the oil in the wok or frying-pan over high heat and add one of the sliced cloves of garlic. Allow to fry until starting to change colour. Add the pork and stir-fry for 40 seconds or until opaque. Remove the pan from the heat and transfer the pork

and garlic to the empty plate, using the perforated spoon (if available). Add the remaining tablespoon of oil to the wok and return it to high heat. Add the rest of the garlic and the ginger and allow to fry until just beginning to change colour. Add the kohlrabi or swede and stir-fry for 1 minute. Add the carrot and stir-fry for another minute. Add the beansprouts and stir-fry for a third minute. Add the stock and stir; add the pork and stir. Stir in the soy and oyster sauces and serve at once.

• SEAFOOD CURRY WITH •
LIME ZEST OR LEMON GRASS

If you use strong chillies with all their seeds, this dish will be very hot; with sweet, moderate ones, it will bring a tingle to the mouth but you will still be able to taste the other ingredients. The chillies are tempered by coconut milk, which brings out the taste of the fish and, in turn, is balanced by the lime zest or lemon grass.

Although the option of lime zest is intended primarily for those who cannot buy fresh lemon grass, I would like to stress that it is a virtually equal alternative: it does not taste the same but suits the curry almost, if not equally, well.

I should perhaps also stress that if young and lightly cooked, squid is sweet and tender: rather than being tough, as I admit it can be, it should have a texture similar to carefully cooked pasta. Choose small fish if possible, so that there are 3 or 4 per 500 g/1 lb, and serve the curry promptly. Most fishmongers will clean the squid for you, but directions for doing it yourself are given below.

Chilled prawns have more flavour than frozen ones; for maximum flavour, buy prawns still in their shells. If you use frozen ones, allow several hours for them to defrost.

For 3–4

• INGREDIENTS •

500 g/1 lb squid

310–400 g/10–13 oz Thai fragrant, Patna or American long-grain white rice

Salt

225 g/7 oz unshelled or 100 g/3½ oz shelled prawns

190 g/6 oz button mushrooms

2–3 sticks celery

50 g/2 oz Kenya or other fine, stringless, green beans

Small bunch coriander leaves (enough for 1 tablespoon when chopped)

1 slim or ½ fat stick lemon grass, or 1 lime (zest only)

3 cloves garlic

2-cm/¾-inch piece fresh root ginger

2 sweet, mild or moderately hot fresh red chillies

½ teaspoon black peppercorns

150 ml/¼ pint coconut milk (see page 24)

2 tablespoons fish sauce

2 tablespoons oil (3 if you use a frying-pan rather than a wok)

Saucepan with a lid (for the rice)
Grater (if substituting lime zest for lemon grass)
Large wok or frying-pan

• METHOD •

1 Clean the squid if necessary. Pull off the head: the innards will come away with it. Discard both, except for the tentacles, which can be used in the curry. Draw out the central bone, or 'pen', which is flat and transparent, rather like a plastic scoop. Peel off the dark skin, wash thoroughly and cut off the fins close to the body. Now turn the fish inside out: fold the flesh at the head back over the body like a sock. The initial folding may need firmness, but after that turning is easy. (The point of this method is that it enables you to clean the inside of the fish without slitting it: thus you can cut it into complete rings.) Wash the inside of the fish, removing any slimy filaments. If it was cleaned by the fishmonger, it should still be washed inside and out in the same manner. Slice the body into rings not more than 5 mm/less than ¼ inch wide. Cut the fins into strips of the same width and about 2.5cm/1 inch long; chop the

tentacles into 2.5-cm/1-inch lengths. Set the prepared squid in a sieve or on a plate lined with kitchen paper to dry.

2 Rinse the rice under the cold tap until the water runs clear, put into the saucepan with a lid and add 600 ml/1 pint salted water for 310 g/10 oz or 800 ml/1⅓ pints for 400 g/13 oz rice. Bring to the boil and stir. Lower the heat, cover and simmer for 12 minutes for Thai rice or 20 minutes for other types of rice. Leave to rest, covered, until the curry is ready.

3 If the prawns are in their shells, pull off the heads of each one and the shell from the tail; pick off the remaining pieces of shell from the body. Wash in cold water. Wash shelled chilled prawns; drain frozen ones. Trim the mushroom stalks; wash, dry and finely slice the mushrooms. Cut off the leaves of the celery, trim the root ends and scrape off any brownish patches. Wash, dry, chop into 2-cm/¾-inch lengths and cross-chop into matchsticks 5 mm/less than ¼ inch wide. Top and tail and wash the beans; cut into 1.5-cm/⅗-inch lengths and leave to drain in a sieve or on a plate lined with kitchen paper.

4 Trim the ends of the coriander stems, wash, shake off surplus moisture and chop finely. Cut off the straw-like leaves from the lemon grass and trim the root, peel off the outer layer and slice into very fine rings (if you use only half a stick, put the spare half into a paper bag and store in the refrigerator). If you are using lime zest, thoroughly wash and finely grate the skin of the lime (green part only). Peel and roughly slice 2 of the cloves of garlic and half the ginger. Trim the stalk ends of the chillies; wash, dry and dice finely. Do not discard the seeds unless you want the curry to be mild. Avoid touching your eyes while handling them and wash your hands directly afterwards. Put the peppercorns into a mortar and crush; add and crush the sliced garlic and ginger. Add the coriander, chillies, lemon grass or lime zest and 1 teaspoon salt and crush to a paste.

5 Peel and finely slice the remaining garlic and ginger, discarding any fibrous patches on the ginger. Check that the beans and squid are dry. Place all the prepared ingredients, plus the coconut milk and fish sauce, within easy reach of the cooker. Warm the oil in the wok or frying-pan over high heat and add the sliced garlic and ginger. Allow to fry for 20–30 seconds, until just starting to change colour. Add the celery and stir for a few seconds; add the beans and stir; add the squid and stir-fry for 30 seconds; add the mushrooms and stir-fry for 1½–2 minutes. Remove the pan from the heat and stir in the paste; return to the heat, add the coconut milk and fish sauce and bring to the boil. Add the prawns, stir gently for 30 seconds–1 minute or until the sauce is slightly reduced, and serve with the rice.

• BRAISED BROCCOLI WITH •
LEMON AND CORIANDER

This is fairly highly flavoured but refreshing. In particular, it would go well with Shehzad's Tandoori-style Chicken (page 106), or Shobhna's Paneer and Tomato Sauce (page 64) or her Saffron Rice with Almonds (page 44). The recipe is adapted from *Anpurna Part* 4 (Shree Oshwal Mahila Mandal).

The dish is simple but you must be careful not to overcook it or to allow it to become dry: if the lemon juice used for steaming evaporates, both the broccoli and the spices will burn.

For 4

• INGREDIENTS •

625 g/1 lb 4 oz broccoli	1 *moderately hot green chilli*
190 g/6 oz (2 medium) tomatoes	4 *tablespoons oil*
2 *teaspoons coriander seeds*	1 *teaspoon cumin seeds*
½ *small lemon*	1 *teaspoon sugar*
2.5-cm/1-inch piece fresh root ginger	Salt

163

Medium-sized saucepan, preferably thick-based, with a close-fitting lid.

• METHOD •

1 Chop the broccoli into florets 3–4 cm/1¼–1½ inches wide at the flower end and 3 cm/1¼ inch long. Wash and leave in a colander to drain. Skin and finely chop the tomatoes (see page 31). Crush the coriander seeds to a fine powder in a mortar; squeeze the lemon. Peel and finely chop the ginger, discarding any fibrous patches. Wash and dry the chilli and trim the stalk end; slit, remove the inner membrane and seeds and dice the flesh very finely. Do not touch your eyes while handling it and wash your hands afterwards.

2 Warm the oil in the saucepan over low heat, add the ginger and allow to fry for 1 minute or until just showing signs of changing colour. Add the chilli and stir. Add the broccoli, cumin (whole), coriander, sugar and a generous pinch of salt and stir-fry gently for 1 minute. Add the tomatoes and stir-fry for 2 minutes; add 1 tablespoon lemon juice, cover and cook for 10–12 minutes (still over low heat). Test the broccoli: it will probably take another 3–4 minutes, but if it is already tender, remove from the heat. If it is not, check that there is still moisture in the bottom of the saucepan, add 1 tablespoon of water if necessary and steam for another minute or two. Test again and, if the broccoli is still hard, steam for a little longer. Serve at once.

• MICHAEL'S ORIENTAL •
FRUIT SALAD

Although sweet dishes are seldom served as a pudding course in China, fruit often follows a dinner in Thailand, where carving and arranging it artistically are part of the national cuisine.

Neither fruit as such nor fruit salads will be cheap, and the recipe below is relatively expensive because of the mango and papaya; however, if you want to keep to the Oriental idiom, you will have to spend a little extra. Do not serve this dish with cream, which would blunt the fresh, intense flavours of the fruit.

It is important that the mango and papaya are ripe. Both should give to the touch without being soft or soft in patches; colour is no guide to ripeness with either, since it depends on type (different varieties of mango are green, yellow and/or deep red, and papayas green, yellow or orange). The kiwi fruit should give slightly to the touch. Choose a navel orange if possible; failing this, it is best to use two small oranges rather than one large one, since small ones tend to be sweeter and juicier.

For 4

• INGREDIENTS •

2 *limes*

25 g/1 *oz caster sugar*

1 *large navel or* 2 *small oranges*

1 *kiwi fruit*

1 *mango*

1 *papaya*

Sharp knife

• METHOD •

1 Squeeze the limes. Add the sugar to the juice and pour into a serving-bowl. Peel the orange, using the sharp knife; take care to trim away all the pith. Cut across into thin slices; halve the slices, removing the pips and fibrous centres. Add to the serving-bowl.

2 Trim the stalk end of the kiwi fruit, peel, slice and add to the bowl. Peel the mango and cut thick slices from each side as far as the stone. Chop the flesh from around the stone; cut into cubes and add. Trim the stalk end of the papaya and peel. Remove the black seeds and cut the flesh into fairly large cubes. Add to the rest of the fruit. Toss gently, cover and chill for 2–3 hours.

• ICE-CREAM •

I have been criticized in the past for including recipes for ice-cream in books which are supposed to be about saving money. However, I make absolutely no apology for giving a couple more here, since nothing is more suitable for serving after an Oriental-style meal, particularly a curry. Ice-cream is also quick and easy to prepare (although the mango one below is less quick than some) and is especially convenient when it comes to giving a party because you can make it days or weeks in advance.

For health reasons, never refreeze ice-cream after defrosting.

• LIME AND MANGO •
ICE-CREAM

The important point about this recipe is that you must choose a ripe mango, not because of flavour, since a less ripe one will give a sharper ice which I personally prefer; however, unless fairly soft, it is very difficult to sieve. When at the right stage, it should give to the touch evenly all over (colour is no guide, as it depends on type rather than maturity).

The time the ice will take to freeze and defrost varies, but for immediate use, allow 2½–3½ hours for freezing and 1–1¼ for defrosting.

You can freeze the ice in a used ice-cream or other plastic container with a fitted lid or in a soufflé-dish or pudding basin covered with foodwrap.

For 4–6

• INGREDIENTS •

1 *ripe mango*

125 *g/4 oz caster sugar*

1 *lime*

50 *ml/¼ pint double cream (not extra-thick)*

Pudding basin or ovenproof dish
Freezer container (if available)
Egg-whisk (if available)

• METHOD •

1 Peel the mango and chop fairly small, cutting around the stone. Put it into a basin with the sugar and leave for 10–15 minutes (this helps to soften the fruit and encourages the juice to run).

2 Press the fruit with the sugar through a moderately fine sieve, using the back of a tablespoon. This takes me a good 15 minutes, but you may be quicker. You should be left with only 1½–2 tablespoons of pulp. Squeeze the lime and stir in the juice. Thoroughly stir in the cream: if it is thick and does not mix smoothly, pass the purée through the sieve.

3 Pour the mixture into a pudding basin or ovenproof dish, cover with foodwrap and freeze for 2–2½ hours or until the edges are frozen but the centre is still soft. Whisk with the egg-whisk, if available; otherwise beat quickly with a fork (if it becomes too warm and reverts to liquid, it defeats the object of beating, which is to improve the texture). Transfer to the freezer container (if available); if you reuse the basin or dish, put the ice-cream into another bowl, wash the basin or dish and cool under the cold tap before drying and refilling. Freeze for 1½–2 hours for eating immediately, or until needed. Before serving, defrost for 1 hour in the refrigerator; beat with a fork just before bringing to the table.

• PISTACHIO MILK ICE •

You can serve this after any Indian-style meal – indeed, after almost any meal at all (I have to admit that pistachio is, without exception, my favourite ice).

As both Kumud and Shehzad stress, it is much lighter and healthier than the Western equivalent because it is made without cream and eggs, thus removing the problem of undercooked eggs in the custard on which this type of ice is usually based. It also makes it cheaper than conventional ice-cream – even with pistachio nuts and vanilla it costs under £2 (exclusive of sugar).

If possible, make it when you are planning to cook something in the oven so that you can crisp the nuts without turning it on specially.

For immediate consumption, allow a total of 2½–3½ hours for freezing (the time varies according to the container and the temperature of the freezer).

For 4

• INGREDIENTS •

8 cardamom pods

1 vanilla pod

900 ml/1½ pints milk

150 g/5 oz caster sugar

75 g/2½ oz shelled pistachio nuts

Small baking-tray (for crisping the nuts; optional)
Egg-whisk (if available)
Small pudding basin or ovenproof dish
Freezer container (if available)

• METHOD •

1 Bruise the cardamoms in a mortar so that the pods are open. Slit the vanilla pod lengthways. Put the milk, sugar, cardamoms and vanilla pod into a saucepan, bring just to the boil and simmer (uncovered) very slowly for 1¼ hours or until the milk is thick, yellow and reduced to about 530 ml/18 fl oz. Allow to cool. Remove the vanilla pod.

2 Pour the flavoured milk through a sieve into the pudding basin or ovenproof dish, cover with foodwrap and freeze for 2–2½ hours or until the milk is frozen stiff round the outside but still liquid in the middle.

3 While the milk freezes, prepare the nuts. Spread them over the baking-tray and bake in the oven for 8 minutes at 180–200°C/350–400°F/Gas Mark 4–6 (the choice of heat is to accommodate whatever else you are cooking). Allow to cool. Crush roughly, leaving some larger pieces.

4 Set the freezer container (if available) to hand. Take the half-frozen ice from the freezer, mix with a fork and whisk until smooth with an egg-whisk (if available); otherwise, beat with the fork. Act quickly to prevent the ice from becoming warm and liquefying. Stir in the nuts, transfer to the freezer container, cover with a lid or foodwrap, and re-freeze. If you are re-using the basin or dish, put the whisked ice-cream into another bowl, quickly wash the basin or dish, cool under the cold tap and dry thoroughly before refilling and refreezing. The ice will be ready to eat in 30 minutes–1 hour; if made in advance, allow 1 hour for defrosting in the refrigerator. Beat with a fork before serving.

· WHEN YOU'RE ·
REALLY BROKE

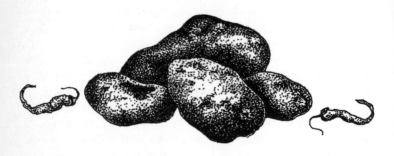

Among the very cheap recipes elsewhere in the book are Lemon and Lentil Soup (page 48); Indian Kedgeree (also made with lentils; page 86); all the recipes for paneer (pages 59–67) and Shehzad's Eggs with Chilli and Coriander (page 75). Chinese omelettes (pages 76–80) are also inexpensive if you fill them simply with a few mushrooms fried with garlic (two cloves) or peas and/or one or two finely sliced spring onions. Another cheap egg dish is Rice and Egg Salad (page 132); Left-over Chicken and Rice Salad costs hardly anything if you have chicken left over from making stock, but as you will probably not make stock when you are broke this dish might be described as economical rather than cheap. The same applies to Lamb Pullao, which is made with stock from the bone of a half leg of lamb.

In this chapter I have given six more inexpensive dishes plus two which are similarly economic. The cheap ones include Shobhna's Yoghurt Sauce; a very simple version of kedgeree which you can serve either with the yoghurt sauce or alone; and two dishes made with potatoes which can be accompanied by plain rice when you are broke or with a variety of Indian-style dishes at other times. The economic recipes are for using up Spiced Rice which, as it is half-way to a pullao, can be turned easily into an excellent stuffing for vegetables. The first, for red peppers, I have included on gastronomic grounds; the second, for courgettes, is cheaper and has the advantage that you need relatively little rice.

The obvious way of using up plain rice is to fry it. I have not given a specific recipe in this chapter (there are several elsewhere in the book), but suggest that you use whatever vegetables you have and add an egg per serving. For frying the vegetables, use the table on page 192; cook the eggs according to the directions for Chinese Omelettes, page 76. Wash, dry and chop the vegetables. Peel and slice 2 or 3 cloves of garlic and a 1.5-cm/⅔-inch piece of root ginger. Make and roll up the omelette, transfer to a plate and chop into 1-cm/½-inch squares. Loosen the rice with a fork and set all the prepared ingredients to hand near the cooker. Warm 2 tablespoons of oil over high heat, fry the garlic and ginger until starting to change colour and stir-fry the vegetables. Lower the heat to medium and stir-fry the rice for 2 minutes, using a wok-scoop or spatula, if available. Add the pieces of egg and stir; add 3 teaspoons of soy sauce per portion, stir and serve.

• CONGEE WITH CARROTS • AND PEAS

In this recipe the rice is cooked in a high proportion of stock to produce a kind of porridge. As relatively little rice is used, the taste of the vegetables comes across surprisingly clearly, so that you may prefer it (as I do) without soy sauce. The small amount of rice, combined with lack of fat, means that the dish is fairly low-calorie; nor is there much besides the peas and spinach to provide protein. Accompany it with plenty of crusty wholemeal bread and make up the protein deficiency at another meal.

Use fresh rather than frozen spinach. When proper spinach is not available, beet spinach, which has larger leaves and thick, white stems, is sometimes sold instead. It does not taste the same as real spinach and cannot always be used in the same way, but is satisfactory in this recipe.

You can make the stock ahead of time, but after the rice is added, the congee must be served when it is ready or the rice will continue to absorb liquid.

For 2–3

• INGREDIENTS •

3 outside sticks celery

310 g/10 oz (5 medium) carrots

150 g/5 oz (1 medium) onion

1 mild green chilli

6 black peppercorns

90 g/3 oz Thai fragrant rice

310 g/10 oz unpodded fresh or 150 g/5 oz frozen peas

1 level teaspoon salt

50 g/2 oz spinach or beet spinach

1 tablespoon soy sauce (optional)

150 ml /¼ pint creamy coconut milk (optional)

Large saucepan

• METHOD •

1 Trim the leaves from the celery; wash the celery and slice fairly thinly. Peel and slice 190 g/6 oz (probably 3) of the carrots. Peel the onion and chop fairly finely. Wash the chilli and slit to expose the seeds (do not remove them); avoid rubbing your eyes while handling it and wash your hands afterwards. Put the prepared vegetables into the large saucepan with the peppercorns and 1.5 litres/2½ pints water, bring just to the boil and simmer for 20–25 minutes. Strain, pressing out as much moisture from the vegetables as possible with the back of a spoon. Throw them away, rinse the saucepan and refill it with the stock.

2 Rinse the rice and add it to the stock. Bring to the boil, stir thoroughly and simmer very gently (uncovered) for 1½ hours, stirring regularly to ensure that the rice does not stick to the bottom of the pan. While it simmers, prepare the rest of the ingredients. Shell the peas if necessary. Put into a saucepan with 370 ml/⅝ pint salted water and boil for 5–15 minutes if fresh or 2 minutes if frozen (the cooking time of fresh ones varies according to age and size). Drain over a bowl to catch the cooking liquor and add the liquor to the congee; reserve the peas. Peel the rest of the carrots and dice into pea-sized

squares. Wash, twice if necessary, and shred the spinach or spinach beet; with beet, cut out and discard the stems.

3 Stir the congee and if it seems very solid, pour in a little water. Add the carrots and salt and simmer for 10 minutes; add the spinach and simmer for 1½–2 minutes, or 2–2½ minutes for beet spinach. Add the peas and simmer for a few seconds. Serve either as it is or with the soy sauce and coconut milk added: the milk will give the congee a rich, creamy taste.

• SHOBHNA'S YOGHURT SAUCE •

This is as near as you can get to the ideal recipe in that it is quick, cheap and healthy. The result is rather like thick slightly tart, spiced cream, with texture added by finely chopped ginger and chillies. It is flavoured just sufficiently to make it interesting without overwhelming the taste of the yoghurt: rather, the yoghurt is enhanced.

For the best flavour, use a yoghurt which is slightly but not very sharp; low-fat is satisfactory but will give a heavier, less creamy result. Chick-pea flour contains more protein than ordinary flour, and can be bought from any good health-food shop.

For 3–4

• INGREDIENTS •

310–450 g/10–14 oz brown or white Patna or American long-grain rice, or Shobhna's Kedgeree (see next recipe) or Spinach Rice (page 40)

Salt

Bunch fresh coriander (enough for 3 tablespoons when chopped); failing coriander, use parsley

2.5-cm/1-inch piece fresh root ginger

2 *green chillies*

450 *g*/14 *oz* (1 *large carton*) *slightly sharp, plain yoghurt*

70 *g*/scant 2½ *oz chick-pea flour*

2 *tablespoons ghee or* 1 *tablespoon ghee plus* 1 *tablespoon oil*

1 *teaspoon cumin seeds*

4 *cloves*

5 *black peppercorns*

10-*cm*/5-*inch stick cinnamon*

4 *bayleaves*

2 *teaspoons or a little more soft dark-brown sugar*

Saucepan with a lid (for the rice)
Egg-whisk
Wok or large saucepan

• METHOD •

1 If serving plain rice, rinse the rice under the cold tap until the water runs clear. Put it into the saucepan with a lid and add 600–900 ml/1–1½ pints water, with some salt if you wish. Bring to the boil, stir, cover and simmer for 20 minutes for white rice or 30 minutes for brown. When it is ready, leave to rest, covered, until the sauce has simmered (see Step 3 below).

2 While the rice cooks, trim the ends of the coriander or parsley stalks; wash the leaves, blot dry with kitchen paper and chop fairly finely. Peel and dice the ginger, rejecting any tough, fibrous patches. Wash and trim the stalk ends of the chillies; slit, remove the inner membrane and all or some of the seeds according to taste and how hot you think they are and chop the flesh finely. Do not touch your eyes while chopping them and wash your hands directly afterwards. (The three chopped ingredients can be put together on the same plate.)

3 Taste the yoghurt to check its sharpness. Mix with the chick-pea flour and add 600 ml/1 pint water. Using the egg-whisk, beat until frothy and smooth. It is important that the flour is completely amalgamated, with no small, unmixed lumps.

4 Put the ghee or ghee and oil into the wok or large saucepan and warm over lowish to medium heat. Throw in the cumin, cloves, peppercorns and cinnamon (all whole); add the bayleaves. Allow to fry for a moment or two, until the cumin seeds start to pop (do not stand over the pan, as they may leap out). Pour in the yoghurt mixture; reduce the heat slightly. Stir continuously until the top of the yoghurt is bubbling (do not let it boil over). Stir in the chopped ginger, chillies and coriander or parsley plus 1 teaspoon salt and the sugar; if the yoghurt is very tart, add a little extra sugar. Reduce the heat until the mixture is just simmering; simmer, without stirring, for 15 minutes. Serve at once, accompanied by Kedgeree or rice.

• SHOBHNA'S KEDGEREE •

This is a perfectly plain lentil dish which can be served either alone or with Shobhna's Yoghurt Sauce (see previous recipe).
   For 3–4

• INGREDIENTS •

250 g/8 oz brown or white Patna or American long-grain rice

190 g/6 oz split-green lentils

Generous pinch salt

Saucepan with a lid

1 teaspoon turmeric

1 small lemon (if to be served alone)

25–40 g/1–1½ oz butter

• METHOD •

1 Rinse the rice and lentils under the cold tap until the water runs clear and put them into the saucepan with a lid. Add 1.35 litres/2¼ pints water (but no salt), bring to the boil, stir and boil briskly for 2 minutes. Lower the heat to a simmer, partially cover (leave a spoon in the saucepan so that the lid is slightly raised) and cook for 25 minutes for white rice or 35 minutes for brown. Add the salt and turmeric and simmer for a further 10 minutes or until both the rice and lentils are very soft. Unless the dish is to be accompanied by yoghurt sauce, cut the lemon into quarters. Stir gently before serving (as the lentils tend to rise to the top). Add a generous knob of butter to each portion and accompany either with yoghurt sauce or lemon wedges.

• LENTILS WITH CORIANDER •

This is made with similar ingredients to Indian Kedgeree (page 86) and is almost as simple. However, the lentils and rice are cooked separately and the lentils simmered with the whole coriander seeds, which are crunchy and, when chewed, have a faint but distinct taste of the leaves.

Serve with Onion Chips (page 27) or Tomato Chutney with Red Pepper (page 30).

For 2–3

• INGREDIENTS •

125 g/4 oz split red lentils

125 g/4 oz brown lentils

250–310 g/8–10 oz (2 medium) onions

90 g/3 oz (1 largish) carrot

6 black peppercorns

4-cm/1½-inch piece fresh root ginger

2 green chillies

2 tablespoons ghee or 3 tablespoons oil

3 teaspoons coriander seeds

1 teaspoon salt

150–225 g/5–7 oz white rice, preferably Basmati

½ lemon

Small saucepan with a lid (for the rice)
Wok or largish saucepan with a lid

• METHOD •

1 Pick over and rinse the lentils. Peel and finely chop the onions; peel and dice the carrot. Crush the peppercorns in a mortar. Peel and roughly chop the ginger, rejecting any fibrous patches; add to the mortar and crush to a paste. Wash and dry the chillies and trim the stalk ends; slit, remove the inner membranes and all or some of the seeds according to how hot you want the dish to be, and dice the flesh as finely as possible. Do not touch your eyes while handling them and wash your hands directly afterwards.

2 Warm the oil or oil and ghee in the wok or largish saucepan over medium heat and fry the onions for 7–8 minutes or until an even gold, turning constantly, especially towards the end. Reduce the heat to low: if the ring responds slowly to a change of setting, remove the pan for a moment or two. Add and stir-fry the lentils and carrot for 3½–4 minutes; stir in the chillies. Add the coriander (whole) with the crushed garlic and peppercorns and stir-fry for a few seconds. Pour in 900 ml/1½ pints water and bring to the boil. Boil briskly for 2 minutes, lower the heat and simmer, covered, for 30 minutes. Add the salt and continue to simmer, covered, for 5–15 minutes or until the brown lentils are tender. (If you want a mushier result, simmer for a little longer.) Leave to rest, covered, for 5–10 minutes. Squeeze the lemon and stir in 3 teaspoons of the juice. Sprinkle with Onion Chips (page 27) or serve with chutney (page 30).

3 Start preparing the rice 5 minutes before you add the salt to the lentils. Rinse under the cold tap until the water runs clear, put into the smaller saucepan with a lid, add a little salt if you wish and pour in 300 ml/½ pint for 150 g/5 oz rice or 450 ml/¾ pint for 225 g/7 oz. Bring to the boil, stir, cover and simmer for 18 minutes for Basmati or 20 minutes for other types of rice. Leave to rest, covered, for 10 minutes. Serve separately.

• SPICED CHICK-PEA •
AND POTATO CAKES

Accompany with rice and Green-Chilli Chutney (page 32) and/or Raita with Cucumber (page 28) when you are broke; at other times, as with Shobhna's Potato Curry (page 182), serve as an additional dish at an Indian-style meal or with chops or an omelette. The cakes can be made up to 24 hours in advance. Use floury potatoes, such as Cara or Maris Piper. You will need stale bread for the breadcrumbs: fresh bread tends to form doughy lumps when grated, and unless the crumbs are fine and uniform the cakes will not brown evenly.

For 3

• INGREDIENTS •

500 g/1 lb floury potatoes

Salt

310–375 g/10–12 oz brown or white Patna or American long-grain rice

Small bunch fresh coriander (enough for 2 tablespoons when chopped)

½ teaspoon cumin seeds

½ teaspoon coriander seeds

¼ teaspoon ground ginger

1½ teaspoons hot chilli powder

1½ teaspoons sugar

190 g/5 oz chick-pea flour

½ lemon

2 tablespoons milk or a little more if needed

50 g/2 oz stale brown or white bread, weighed without crust

5-6 tablespoons oil

Saucepan with a lid (for the rice)
Smallish baking-tray (if you want to cook the cakes in the oven)
Wok or frying-pan (if you want to fry the cakes)

• METHOD •

1 Peel the potatoes, removing any green patches. Cut into even-sized pieces, just cover with slightly salted water and boil for 15–20 minutes or until soft. Mash with a fork.

2 Rinse the rice until the water runs clear and put into the saucepan with a lid. Add 600 ml/1 pint water for 310 g/10 oz rice or 750 ml/1¼ pints for 375 g/12 oz; add a little salt if you wish. Bring to the boil, stir, cover and simmer for 20 minutes for white rice or 30 minutes for brown. Leave to rest, covered, for 10 minutes.

3 Trim the ends of the coriander stems; wash, blot dry and chop finely. Crush the cumin and coriander seeds to a powder in a mortar. Mix together the coriander seeds and leaves, cumin,

ginger, hot chilli powder, sugar, ½ teaspoon salt and 125 g/ 4 oz of the chick-pea flour. Squeeze the lemon. Mash the flour and flavourings with 1 tablespoon lemon juice into the potato. Add as much milk as is needed to form a firm dough. Mould into 6 flat cakes.

4 Finely grate the bread. Spread out the breadcrumbs on a large plate. Pour 2 tablespoons oil on to a second plate. Spread the remaining 25 g/1 oz chick-pea flour over the bottom of a third plate. Roll the cakes first in the flour, then in the oil, then in the breadcrumbs; press the crumbs firmly in place to make sure that they stick and shake off any surplus. If you are making the cakes in advance, cover and store in the refrigerator.

5 The cakes can be either fried or baked. To bake, pre-heat the oven to 225°C/450°F/Gas Mark 7 and line the baking-tray with cooking-foil. Spread 3–4 tablespoons oil over the tray, add the cakes and turn so that each side is coated. Bake for 10–15 minutes or until the underside is deep golden; then turn and bake for a further 5–7 minutes or until the second side is golden brown. To fry, warm 3 tablespoons oil in a wok or frying-pan over lowish heat and fry for 3 minutes or until gold, turning once or twice. Serve with the rice.

• SHOBHNA'S SPICED BATTER •

Shobhna, who comes Gujarat in the north of India, is a Jain. Jainism is a belief which sprang from the same roots as Buddhism but is older, and also stricter, at any rate with regard to *ahimsa*. This is the tenet that one should not kill anything: thus Jains are rigorous vegetarians and do not eat eggs (as an embryo lives), although they are permitted milk and milk products. In fact, this batter contains neither eggs nor milk but is made from high-protein chick-pea flour flavoured with spices and moistened with lemon juice and water. You can use it to make paneer or various vegetable fritters, which can be eaten as snacks or the first course to a meal or as part of a main course with Spiced Rice (page 39), Shobhna's Spinach Rice (page 40), or Saffron Rice with Almonds (page 40). The most popular sort of vegetable fritter is onion, but I think broccoli works even better, although broccoli florets do not look so attractive as onion rings; other suitable vegetables are cauliflower and sweet potato. (If, however, you serve vegetable fritters and Spiced Rice, as opposed to paneer fritters or Saffron Rice, bear in mind that despite the chick-pea flour you will be eating relatively little protein.)

Either serve the fritters directly after frying or fry them an hour or so in advance and reheat them in the oven. Once they have cooled, the moisture in the filling causes them to lose their crispness fairly quickly.

You will need a smallish to medium-sized saucepan for frying. In order to save oil the saucepan should not be large, but it must be big enough to cover the source of heat, since hot oil is very inflammable and it is essential for safety to ensure that if any splutters or spills it will not come into contact with the flame.

Makes 16–25 fritters

• INGREDIENTS •

Bunch coriander (enough for 2 tablespoons when chopped; optional)

1 *teaspoon cumin seeds*

8 *black peppercorns*

1 *teaspoon salt*

2.5-cm/1-inch piece *fresh root ginger*

1 *teaspoon hot chilli powder*

½ *teaspoon ground turmeric*

Pinch *of sugar*

75 g/2½ oz *chick-pea flour*

200–250 g/6½–8 oz *paneer, moulded into 15–16 balls (see page 62), or sweet potato, broccoli and/or cauliflower, or 2 medium onions*

½ *lemon*

½ *teaspoon bicarbonate of soda*

330–450 ml/11–15 fl oz *corn oil*

4–5 *small cubes of stale bread (for testing the temperature of the oil)*

Smallish to medium-sized thick-based saucepan
Perforated spoon
Largish baking-tray (for reheating the fritters)

• METHOD •

1 If you are serving the fritters with Spiced, Spinach or Saffron Rice, time Spiced Rice to be ready or put Spinach Rice in the oven before you heat the oil for frying (see Step 5); finish Saffron Rice as soon as the fritters are fried.

2 Trim the ends of the coriander stalks; wash, blot dry and chop finely. Crush the cumin and peppercorns (and the salt if in flakes) to a fine powder in a mortar (thorough crushing of all the ingredients for the batter is necessary to give a smooth result). Peel and roughly slice the ginger, rejecting any fibrous patches. Add to the mortar and pound to a paste. Add the coriander and crush as thoroughly as possible. Stir in the chilli powder, turmeric and sugar and transfer to a bowl. Add and stir in the chick-pea flour plus 3 tablespoons of water. Mix to a completely smooth, thick paste, pressing out lumps of flour against the side of the bowl. Then stir in another 1½ tablespoons water (I suggest adding only 3 tablespoons to start with because it is easier to press out lumps when the mixture is very stiff). Cover with a plate and leave to rest while you prepare the filling or for at least 15 minutes.

3 Make paneer balls (see page 62) or prepare vegetables. Peel and finely slice onions; peel and thinly slice sweet potato. Wash broccoli or cauliflower and cut into florets about 2 cm/¾ inch long at the flower end: if larger, they may still be a little crunchy after frying. Blot dry with kitchen paper.

4 About 5 minutes before heating the oil for frying, stir the lemon juice into the batter. If the batter is still very solid, add just a little more water: it should be thick but not so thick that it will not drop from a spoon. Add and stir in the bicarbonate of soda. The soda will fizz at first but soon subside. The reason for using it is that it puffs up the fritters and makes them light and crisp: without it, they will be flaccid even when hot. Immerse as many paneer balls or pieces of vegetable in the batter as you can ideally they should all soak in it for a few minutes before cooking, but if they will not all fit into the bowl at once, you can add the rest as you fry.

5 Pour corn oil into the smallish saucepan to a depth of at least 5 cm/2 inches. Set over medium heat for 4–5 minutes. Meanwhile set a large plate lined with kitchen paper to hand near the cooker. When the oil has been heating for about 4 minutes, test its temperature by lowering one of the cubes of bread into it: take care to add it slowly so that the oil does not splutter (this also applies to putting in the fritters). If the bread is fried gold in 40 seconds (count to 40), it has reached about 190°C/375°F, which is the correct heat for deep-frying. To maintain this temperature, reduce the heat to fairly low.

6 Pick up one of the pieces of filling with the perforated spoon, hold it over the batter so that any surplus will fall back into the bowl, then lower it into the oil. After about 20 seconds, repeat: continue until there are 6 or 8 in the pan. They should be added one at a time at short intervals to prevent the temperature of the oil from dropping. Cook each for about 2 minutes or until slightly puffed up and mid-golden-brown; when cooked, set on the paper-lined plate to drain. Replace each with the next as soon as it is fried; similarly, put any uncoated pieces of filling into the batter as the bowl empties. If for immediate consumption, serve as soon as you have finished frying; if you are making the fritters in advance, leave on the plate until cold and cover. Reheat on a baking-tray, covered with cooking-foil, in a pre-heated oven at 190°C/375°F/Gas Mark 5 for 7–10 minutes. Keep a watchful eye on paneer fritters, since if baked for too long the cheese will melt and may start to ooze out of its coating.

• SHOBHNA'S POTATO CURRY •

The recipe Shobhna gave me contains only potato: I have added eggs, which she, as a Jain, does not eat. The eggs enrich the flavour and make the dish into a complete meal. However, when you are not broke you could serve it without them, not only as an accompaniment at an Indian-style meal but also with plain grilled meat or omelettes. If you make it without eggs, use 1 kg/2 lb potatoes (do not alter the quantities of the other ingredients); as a vegetable, it will be enough for 4.

Use waxy potatoes (such as Pentland Javelin, Maris Bard or Maris Peer): floury ones may crumble.

Serve with Tomato Chutney with Red Pepper.

For 3

• INGREDIENTS •

250–310 g/8–10 oz white Patna or American long-grain rice

Salt

750 g/1½ lb waxy potatoes

250 g/8 oz fresh, ripe or tinned tomatoes

Few coriander leaves (optional)

3 eggs

4 tablespoons oil

¼ teaspoon black mustard seeds

1¼ teaspoons cumin seeds

1 teaspoon coriander seeds

¼ teaspoon ground ginger

½ teaspoon ground turmeric

¼ teaspoon hot chilli powder

Saucepan with a lid (for the rice)
Largish saucepan or wok with a lid

• METHOD •

1 Rinse the rice under the cold tap until the water runs clear and put into the saucepan with a lid. Add 500 ml/⅚ pint water for 250 g/8 oz or 600 ml/1 pint for 310 g/10 oz rice; add salt if you wish. Bring to the boil, stir, cover and simmer for 20 minutes. Leave to stand, covered, for at least 10 minutes.

2 Peel the potatoes, removing any green patches just under the skin and chop into 1-cm/½-inch cubes. If using fresh tomatoes, skin them (see page 31) and chop fairly finely, discarding the hard cores. If using coriander leaves, trim the ends of the stems, wash, shake dry and chop coarsely.

3 Set the eggs to boil; boil for 12 minutes. Leave until cool enough to handle or immerse briefly in cold water. Shell and chop into pieces about the same size as the potatoes.

4 Warm the oil in the largish saucepan or wok over medium/low heat and add the mustard seeds. When they pop, add the cumin. Stir and add the potatoes. Stir again, add 4 tablespoons water and cook for 10 minutes, stirring frequently; add the coriander seeds, ginger, turmeric, chilli powder, 1 teaspoon salt and the tomatoes. Cover and cook for another 6–7 minutes, stirring gently now and again. Add the eggs and continue to cook for another 1–2 minutes or until the potatoes are tender; if the pan becomes dry, add just a little more water. Sprinkle with the fresh coriander, if using, and serve.

• Using up Left-over • Spiced Rice

On the assumption that you will have only a little, I suggest using up left-over Spiced Rice to stuff vegetables. You may feel that the following recipe for red pepper is not ideal in this chapter because the peppers are relatively dear; courgettes, however, are cheaper, especially in the autumn.

If you are in a hurry, you can omit the onion and garlic in both recipes, which cuts out frying, but the result will be less interesting. For a crunchy texture, crisp the nuts in the oven before adding them to the stuffing: put them in a small baking-dish and toast for 5–6 minutes.

Neither dish supplies much protein: make up the deficiency at another meal.

• Stuffed Red Peppers •

I personally do not like the peppers unskinned: you may mind less.

Serve with Raita with Cucumber (see page 28), bread and, if possible, crudités (see page 133).

For 2 or 4; if for 4, you will need plenty of bread

• INGREDIENTS •

4 red peppers	1 tablespoon oil
20 g/¾ oz sultanas	25 g/1 oz unsalted peanuts
150–190 g/5–6 oz unpodded fresh or 75–90 g/2½–3 oz frozen peas	25 g/1 oz cashew nuts or almonds
Salt	190 g/6 oz cooked Spiced Rice (see page 39)
125 g/4 oz (1 smallish) onion	½ lemon
2 cloves garlic	

Shallow ovenproof dish, ideally 16–18cm/6½–7 inches across
Wok or frying-pan

• METHOD •

1 Skin the peppers (see page 31). It is decidedly preferable
to skin them over a gas burner if you can, because they will be
less cooked and the flesh firmer. After skinning, cut off the
tops, remove the core and use a teaspoon to scoop out the
seeds. Reserve the juice inside to mix with the filling.

2 Soak the sultanas in cold water for 10–15 minutes; drain.
Shell the peas if necessary; just cover with slightly salted
water and cook for 2 minutes if frozen or 5–15 minutes if fresh
(the time they take is very variable). Peel and finely chop the
onion and garlic.

3 Pre-heat the oven to 200°C/400°F/Gas Mark 6; lightly grease
the ovenproof dish. Warm the oil in the wok or frying-pan over
medium heat and fry the onion for 2 minutes or until
beginning to change colour, turning frequently. Add the garlic
and fry for a few seconds; add the nuts and turn in the oil.
Remove from the heat. Mix the contents of the pan with the
peas, sultanas, fried rice and juice from the peppers.

4 Stuff the peppers, taking care not to split them (this applies
especially if they were skinned by grilling or baking). Place
them upright in the dish: a dish of the size given will support
them, but they will usually stand upright without difficulty.
Sprinkle a little lemon juice over each (squeeze straight from
the lemon) and bake for 10–15 minutes. Serve immediately.

• STUFFED COURGETTES •

Serve with Raita with Cucumber (see page 28).
For 4

• INGREDIENTS •

*As above except that you will need
8 courgettes weighing about 125 g/
4 oz each instead of peppers,*

*30 g/generous 1 oz sultanas and
1 moderately hot green chilli*

Large saucepan
Largish, shallow ovenproof dish

• METHOD •

1 Trim the ends of the courgettes, wash and put into the large saucepan (if necessary, trim a little extra from the ends to make them fit). Cover with slightly salted water, bring to the boil and boil for 6–7 minutes. Drain, turn into a colander and refresh (see page 16) in cold water. Leave to cool a little. Slit in half lengthways and cut around the insides 7 mm/⅓ inch from the skin and ends and about half the courgette deep. Using a teaspoon pull or scoop out the flesh inside the cut. Turn the shells upside-down to drain and chop the scooped-out flesh fairly finely.

2 Prepare the sultanas, peas, onion and garlic as above. Wash and dry the chilli and trim the stalk end; slit, remove the inner membrane and seeds, and dice the flesh as finely as possible. Do not touch your eyes while handling it and wash your hands afterwards.

3 Pre-heat the oven to 200°C/400°F/Gas Mark 6. Continue as for previous Step 3, adding the chilli to the pan at the same time as the nuts. Mix the chopped courgette flesh with the stuffing.

4 Lightly oil the ovenproof dish and arrange the courgette shells over the bottom. Put as much stuffing as they will hold into each and distribute the rest between them or on top. Sprinkle with lemon juice as before and cover the dish with cooking-foil. Bake in the oven for 12 minutes; remove the foil and bake for 5 minutes more. When serving, try not to break the shells (the easiest implement to use, if inelegant, is a fish-slice or spatula). Serve at once.

· NUTRITION ·

Five types of nutrient are needed for health: carbohydrates which include both starches and sugars; fats and oils; proteins; vitamins; and minerals. In addition, your food should provide a moderate, but not excessive, amount of fibre.

Carbohydrates supply energy. As sugars contribute nothing except calories, and dental decay is caused by added sugar (as opposed to that which is naturally present in produce such as fruit), most of your energy requirements should be met by starchy foods. These also supply other nutrients. For example, white flour is 77% starch and wholemeal 63%, but they also contain 10% and 13% respectively of protein, plus iron, calcium and B vitamins. White rice is 86% starch and 7% protein; brown 8% protein, with B vitamins, a little calcium and a very little iron. A healthy proportion of starch in your diet is about 35% of total calorie intake.

Fats and Oils provide a more concentrated form of energy. They consist chiefly of a number of fatty acids. Some fatty acids are saturated – that is stable – some monounsaturated and some polyunsaturated. All fats and oils are composed of a mixture, but milk, cheese, butter, beef and chocolate contain a high proportion of saturated and a very low proportion of polyunsaturated fats. Vegetable oils have a higher proportion of poly- or monounsaturated. You are recommended to eat not more than 35% of total calories in the form of fat or oil and not more than 10% in the form of saturated fat.

Proteins are essential for the growth and maintenance of the body; they may also be burnt as energy. They consist of chains of amino acids which can vary almost infinitely in order and proportion. Those contained in plant proteins are less like those in humans than animal proteins and less useful when eaten singly, but can be given greater value if two or more are combined at the same meal. The value of the protein in rice, for example, is increased when it is accompanied by that from peas or lentils.

Anyone trying to lose weight should note that if you do not eat enough carbohydrate and fat to fulfil your energy needs, protein can be used instead, which might lead to a lack of protein for repair of tissues, even though you are eating the recommended amount.

The estimated average daily needs of energy and protein given in the Department of Health's *Dietary Reference Values for Food, Energy and Nutrients* (1991) are:

	Kcal	Protein
18-year-olds		
Boys	2,755	46 g
Girls	2,110	37 g
19–49-year-olds		
Men	2,550	44 g
Women	1,940	36 g

As individual protein requirements vary, you are advised to eat a little more than the average daily requirement: 55 g are recommended for men in the 19–49-year-old age-group and 45 g for women.

To illustrate this in terms of meals, a portion of Almond Pullao with Red Pepper and Peas would supply about 23 g of protein, with 7 g from the rice, 7 g from the peas and 9 g from the nuts. The rest of the day's quota could come from a size 2 egg (about 8 g), a moderate serving of muesli (about 5 g) and 300 ml/½ pint milk (9 g), plus a piece of cheese for men (40 g/1½ oz Cheddar contains about 10 g). If you do not eat as much as this on one day, it does not matter so long as you make it up on another: it is average intake that counts.

Vitamins perform various functions: vitamin A is needed for healthy skin and eyes; the B vitamins (which are a group) are needed for metabolizing components of food and, in the case of vitamin B12, for preventing anaemia and keeping nerve cells healthy; vitamin C promotes healing; and vitamin D maintains levels of calcium and phosphorus in the blood. Sources of vitamin A include milk products, eggs, carrots and yellow or dark-green vegetables; sources of vitamin B include, milk, eggs, meat and offal and, in the cast of vitamin B12, fermented foods such as yeast and soy products; sources of vitamin C are fruit and vegetables, notably green peppers and citrus fruit; and sources of vitamin D include animal foods, although most people gain as much as they need from sunlight.

Minerals are similarly needed for many purposes, including the formation of bones and teeth and to regulate body cells and fluids. Fifteen or more are required altogether, but the major ones are: iron, calcium, phosphorus, magnesium, sodium and chlorine, and potassium. Sources of iron include milk, meat, eggs, bread, aubergines, potatoes, chocolate and curry powder. Sources of calcium are milk products, eggs, fish, beef, watercress, onions and peanuts. Phosphorus and magnesium are contained in most foods, but notably in brown bread and peanuts; sodium and chlorine are found in salty foods; and potassium in many foods but, in particular, raisins, instant coffee, yeast products and potato crisps.

Fibre comes from plant cellulose: whole-grain products contain more than white products but you do not need large amounts.

CHART OF FOOD VALUES

Figures from: unmarked, *Manual of Nutrition* (HMSO, 1985 edition); marked*, McCance and Widdowson, *The Composition of Foods* (Royal Society of Chemistry and Ministry of Agriculture, Fisheries & Food, 1991 edition); marked **, manufacturers' packages; N=nutrient present in significant amounts but reliable data not available. All values are for 100 g.

	Energy kcal	Protein g	Fat g	Carbo g
• MEAT				
Beef*,				
* lean only, raw (average)*	123	20.3	4.6	0
Rump steak*,				
* lean only, grilled*	168	28.6	6.0	0
Chicken,				
* roast, without skin*	148	24.8	5.4	0
Lamb*,				
* lean only, roast leg*	191	29.4	8.1	0
Pork*,				
* lean only, raw (average)*	147	20.7	7.1	0
• FISH				
Cod*, raw	76	17.4	0.7	0
Haddock*, raw	73	16.8	0.6	0
Prawns*, boiled	107	22.6	1.8	0
• DAIRY PRODUCTS & EGGS				
Butter	740	0.4	82.0	0
Cream (double)	447	1.5	48.2	2.0
Cream (single)	195	2.4	19.3	3.2
Eggs**, size 2	144	12.3	10.5	tr
Fromage frais*, plain	113	6.8	7.1	5.7
Milk (whole)	65	3.2	3.9	4.6
Milk (skimmed)	32	3.4	0.1	4.7
• GROCERIES				
Chilli powder*	N	12.3	16.8	N

Cinnamon*	N	3.9	3.2	N
Fish sauce**	257	12.5	tr	2.6
Flour (white)**	340	9.9	1.4	72.0
Flour (wholemeal)	306	12.7	2.2	62.8
Oil (groundnut)**	824	<0.1	91.6	0
Rice (brown)**, boiled	135	2.7	1.1	28.6
Rice (white)**, boiled	121	2.7	0.4	26.6
Soy sauce	56	5.2	0.5	8.3
Sugar (white)**	400	0.0	0.0	100

• NUTS

Almonds	565	16.9	53.5	4.3
Cashew nuts*, roasted	611	20.5	50.9	18.8
Coconut*, desiccated	669	6.0	68.8	7.0
Peanuts, shelled, plain*	564	25.6	46.1	12.5
Pistachio nuts*, unshelled	331	9.9	30.5	4.6

• PULSES & TOFU

Chick peas*, raw	320	21.3	5.4	49.6
Kidney beans, red, raw	272	22.1	1.7	45.0
Lentils*, raw	297	24.3	1.9	48.8
Tofu**	73	8.1	4.2	0.7

• VEGETABLES

Aubergine	14	0.7	0	3.1
Beans, French*	24	1.9	0.5	3.2
Beansprouts (mung)*, raw	31	2.9	0.5	4.0
Carrots*, old, raw	35	0.6	0.3	7.9
Cauliflower, boiled	9	1.6	0	0.8
Celery*, raw	7	0.5	0.2	0.9
Chillies & peppers*, green, raw	20	2.9	0.6	0.7
Chillies & peppers*, red, raw	32	1.0	0.4	6.4
Courgettes, raw	29	1.6	0.4	5.0
Cucumber	10	0.6	0.1	1.8
Garlic*, raw	98	7.9	0.6	16.3
Lettuce	12	1.0	0.4	1.2
Mange-tout peas*	32	3.6	0.2	4.2
Mushrooms	13	1.8	0.6	0
Onion	23	0.9	0	5.2
Peas, frozen, boiled	72	6.0	0.9	10.7

Potatoes, early new*	70	1.7	0.3	16.1
Potatoes, old*	75	2.1	0.2	17.2
Spinach, boiled	30	5.1	0.5	1.4
Swede*, raw	24	0.7	0.3	5.0
Sweetcorn on cob*, boiled	66	2.5	1.4	11.6
Tomatoes	14	2.9	0	2.8

● **FRUIT**

Grapes	63	0.6	0	16.1
Lemon juice	7	0.3	0	1.6
Mango	59	0.5	0	15.3
Oranges	35	0.8	0	8.5
Pears	41	0.3	0	10.6

VEGETABLE & TOFU STIR-FRYING TIMES

Aubergines: 4–5 minutes
Beans (stringless): 2–3 minutes
Beansprouts: 1–3 minutes
Broccoli: boil 2 minutes, stir-fry 2–3 minutes
Cabbage: boil 2 minutes, stir-fry 1–2 minutes
Carrots: 2–3 minutes
Cauliflower: boil 2 minutes, stir-fry 2–3 minutes
Celeriac: 2–3 minutes
Celery: 2–3 minutes
Chillies (finely chopped): 30 seconds–1 minute
Courgettes: 2–3 minutes
Mange-tout peas: 1–2 minutes
Mushrooms: 1–2 minutes
Onions: 2–3 minutes
Parsnip: 2–3 minutes
Pepper (green): 2–3 minutes
Pepper (red): 4–5 minutes
Spinach: 1–2 minutes
Tofu (to be crisp): 3–5 minutes
Turnip: 2–3 minutes

Broad beans, peas, potatoes, red cabbage, spinach beet leaves, sweetcorn and tomatoes are unsuitable for stir-frying.

• INDEX •